DESIGN LEADERSHIP IGNITED

DESIGN

LEADERSHIP

IGNITED

ELEVATING DESIGN AT SCALE

ERIC QUINT
GERDA GEMSER
GIULIA CALABRETTA

STANFORD BUSINESS BOOKS
An Imprint of Stanford University Press
Stanford, California

Stanford University Press
Stanford, California

Special discounts for bulk quantities of Stanford Business Books are available to corporations, professional associations, and other organizations. For details and discount information, contact the special sales department of Stanford University Press. Tel: (650) 725-0820, Fax: (650) 725-3457

Printed in the United States of America on acid-free, archival-quality paper

Library of Congress Cataloging-in-Publication Data

Names: Quint, Eric, author. | Gemser, Gerda, author. | Calabretta, Giulia, author.
Title: Design leadership ignited : elevating design at scale / Eric Quint, Gerda Gemser, and Giulia Calabretta.
Description: Stanford, California : Stanford Business Books, an Imprint of Stanford University Press, 2022. | Includes bibliographical references and index.
Identifiers: LCCN 2021016686 (print) | LCCN 2021016687 (ebook) | ISBN 9781503613966 (cloth) | ISBN 9781503629868 (ebook)
Subjects: LCSH: Leadership. | Industrial design—Management.
Classification: LCC HD57.7 .Q567 2022 (print) | LCC HD57.7 (ebook) | DDC 658.5/752—dc23
LC record available at https://lccn.loc.gov/2021016686
LC ebook record available at https://lccn.loc.gov/2021016687

Cover illustration: iStock
Figure and table design: Joe Kral
Developmental editor: Jianne Whelton
Typeset by Newgen North America in 10/15 Spectral

Contents

Contents

Preface

WHY THIS BOOK WITH THESE AUTHORS

This book is the result of a shared interest in effective design leadership and how to master it within complex and ever-changing organizations. During the course of their academic careers, Gerda and Giulia have completed numerous studies on design management, done research with industry partners, published extensively on design management, and lectured at leading design and business schools. Eric, on the other hand, has a long-standing and successful professional design career that includes several executive design leadership roles in companies renowned for their design and innovation track record, including Royal Philips and 3M Company. His achievements have been cited and featured in a number of books and international publications, and Eric is a frequent guest lecturer and keynote speaker on design leadership, brand, and innovation.

In hindsight, it makes perfect sense for these three authors to collaborate on the subject matter in this book. Gerda and Giulia had originally intended to write an academic paper on effective design leadership, and to this end, they interviewed many practitioners who occupied senior design leadership roles at the time. As part of this research, they also asked Eric about the practices, methods, and approaches he considered essential for effective design leadership. The transcript of Eric's replies revealed that there was so much more he could share about design leadership and that the one interview with him had only scratched the surface. During one of the conversations that followed, Eric mentioned that he had been wondering for a while when the opportunity would arise for him to capture his experiences in a book on design leadership. This made Gerda and Giulia ask themselves whether they should pivot and write a book together with Eric instead. A book — particularly one published by a reputable publisher like Stanford University Press — could potentially reach a much wider audience than an academic article. Gerda and Giulia had gained some interesting insights during interviews they had conducted with several senior design leaders for their academic research. But these interviews were usually one-time, one-hour sessions; the idea of being able to write a book with Eric, and tap into his knowledge and experience in an unlimited way, was extremely appealing. The possibility of working with Gerda and Giulia was equally attractive to Eric, as it offered an opportunity to enrich his perspectives and reflect on his professional experience from a more academic point of view. On the basis of these considerations, the three authors decided to join forces and embark on the journey of writing a book on design leadership together.

Design Leadership Ignited is the fruit of the combined efforts of its authors. It provides practical guidance to (aspiring) design leaders grounded on the authors' combined expertise and ongoing exchanges, the content and analysis of Gerda's and Giulia's interviews with senior design leaders, a deep dive into relevant professional and academic publications, and Eric's extensive and practical design experience as an executive design leader in complex business environments.

The main aim of the book is to provide readers with practical advice about design leadership, including several approaches to different facets of it — and with this, to inspire the next generation of design leaders to become more knowledgeable and confident, and hence better at what they do. Beyond the practical nature of this work, the authors offer their reflections on and deeper insights into design leadership more generally. The basic premise is that design leadership is all about navigating contradictory imperatives, for example consolidation versus change, or conventionality versus novelty. The overarching lens used in this book is congruent with what is known as a pragmatic, antidualism perspective, which has been formulated in certain academic works on management. This integrative perspective avoids a one-sided focus on one particular aspect over another. With this book, design professionals are encouraged to embrace complexity and resolve seemingly opposing challenges when engaged in leadership. Embracing the complexity of design leadership, rather than getting distracted and made ineffective by it, will elevate design at scale.

Acknowledgments

We would like to thank our colleagues and peers who contributed to the writing of this book on design leadership. The book would not have been possible without their inspiration, advice, and support. In particular, our gratitude goes out to the many design leaders interviewed for sharing their rich experiences; to the editorial and production team at Stanford University Press for recognizing the value of this book and for assisting in the publishing process; and to the reviewers of the manuscript for their constructive feedback that resulted in a better book.

Finally, we would like to offer a heartfelt thanks to our families and friends for offering their never-ending support in so many ways — but most especially, for engaging in endless conversations on a topic that we are so passionate about: design leadership. Without this support, we could never have overcome the unique challenge of working from home across three different continents and three different time zones. In the end, the realization of this book was a truly global collaboration — an act of creativity and design with everyone involved.

Eric, Gerda, and Giulia

CHAPTER 1

Design Context

*Elevating design at scale throughout an organization
is a quest for inclusion at every level. It requires "ignited"
design leadership to engage effectively with business
leaders and drive transformation together.*

DESIGN OFFERS ORGANIZATIONS an opportunity to enhance brand experience, advance innovation, and drive transformation and progress towards more desirable futures. As a result, an increasing number of organizations are investing in growing their in-house design teams and extending the influence and ownership of design to their executive level. Examples of well-known companies that were among the first to elevate design to the C-suite level and appoint a chief design officer (CDO) include Philips, PepsiCo, 3M Company, Johnson & Johnson, and Apple.

Leading the design function inside an organization is, however, a complex task, particularly if the organization is not well-versed with design as a driver for business value. If the design function is not effectively led, it can result in suboptimal organizational outcomes. This, ultimately, impacts the credibility of and investment in the design function going forward.

The aim of this book, therefore, is to

- *ground existing design leaders* in practices, frameworks, and tools they can use to effectively lead the design function within their organizations;

- *enable upcoming design leaders* to better prepare for their future (executive) design leadership role, making them more knowledge-able and confident in their ability to fulfill this role successfully;
- *inform business leaders* about the scope of design and how to partner with design in order to maximize its business value and impact;
- *support (design) consultants* when they advise their clients on how to build and lead an in-house design function;
- *assist design (leadership) educators* in their efforts to provide students with state-of-the art knowledge on design leadership — knowledge gained from experienced design leaders;
- *inspire (design) students* to explore the field of design leadership and envision a possible career path in this area.

This book provides insights and guidelines into how to lead an in-house design function. Ignited design leadership "elevates design at scale" by guaranteeing that organizations maximize the full potential design can offer them. Organizations with an in-house design function are in general mid-sized to large, and may have complex, matrix-type organizational structures covering different businesses, functions, and geographies. Within these organizations, design leadership happens at different levels. In this book, the term *executive design leader* is used to refer to the head of the design function, the person who occupies the most senior role within the organization's hierarchy in terms of design. The term *design leader* is used to refer to the people who lead design efforts for a particular business unit, function, or region of an organization. Our guidelines and frameworks are aimed at both types of leaders. Together these design leaders form the design leadership team, which is responsible for delivering design excellence across the organization.

In complex, large organizations, design leaders have to navigate within multiple layers of management and will be confronted with priorities that may conflict and will need to be aligned across various organizational entities. Leaders will have to contend with formalized routines and processes that affect their ability to act in a dynamic way. Indeed, a core challenge to successful design leadership is the ability to effectively manage dualities — objectives or activities that are inherently contradictory in some way. For example, to drive sustainable competitive advantage in a rapidly evolving environment, design leaders need to act as change agents and use creativity to encourage organizations to do things differently. On the other hand, to enact viable business outcomes design leaders also need to exploit existing resources, processes, and business directions by doing more of the same — only better. Leading a design function requires navigating these potential dualities. This book provides insights and guidelines on how to do so effectively.

Design Leadership Ignited is the collaborative effort of two academics (Gerda and Giulia) and an industry practitioner (Eric) and is the result of a shared interest in effective design leadership and how to master it within complex and ever-changing organizations. Gerda and Giulia have published extensively on design management and lectured on this topic at leading design and business schools. Eric, on the other hand, has a long-standing professional design career that includes several executive design leadership roles in companies renowned for their design and innovation track record, including Royal Philips and 3M Company. The insights in this book are based on the knowledge and experiences gained by the authors during the course of their careers and interviews conducted with fifty-nine design leaders. Of the design leaders interviewed, 54 percent acted at executive level (having the title of CDO, Head of Design, (S)VP of Design, or similar) and the remaining 46 percent at a senior design leadership level (having the title of Design Director or similar). The organizations these design leaders work for are predominantly for-profit organizations that cover a broad range of different industries from (fast moving) consumer goods to industrial supplies, finance, consulting, health, IT services, and many more. Their organizations were (at the time) generally larger-sized (a thousand employees or more), operating on a global scale in B2B and/or B2C markets, and had their headquarters in Europe (34 percent), the USA (50 percent), or the Asia Pacific region (16 percent). Throughout the book, quotes from the interviews conducted are used to illustrate or emphasize particular arguments.[1] More details on the research method can be found in "Appendix: Research Method and Approach."

DESIGN LEADERSHIP IGNITED

Effective design leadership is essential to establish, empower, and elevate design for excellence at scale. Although design leadership shares many similar characteristics with regular business and functional leadership roles related to people, financial, or strategic management, leading a team of highly creative professionals comes with some unique characteristics and challenges. For example, designers tend to be quite comfortable with the unknown and have a passion for attaining meaningful outcomes that needs to be carefully nurtured.[2]

Design leadership builds a bridge between business and design while also creating an environment in which the design team can thrive. Design leadership is not about designing products or services but is about enabling the organization to design products and services. Eric suggested that as a design leader "[y]ou represent creativity and design as a functional leader for the company, and your mission to bring design to the world, and the world to design."[3]

The subtitle of this book is "Elevating Design at Scale." This will require design leaders to demonstrate their capacity and experience as change agents, ability to engage with business leadership, and skill at leading a high-performing design team to maximize the full potential of design. This challenge was aptly described metaphorically by the global design leader of a home appliances company:

> After school, like so many fledgling designers, I came into the corporation with all these ideals, and tried to implement them . . . but then you notice that the corporation is actually one "giant container floating in the ocean" and you have to work with very long[term] time frames, like planning months in advance, while in a smaller design studio, it's a little bit more flexible and versatile.

Elevating design at scale refers to growing the design function in terms of the quantity of its activities and the quality of its outcomes. From a quantitative perspective, design at scale might relate to optimizing the number of designers employed within the design function overall or within various business units, and the number of satellite design studios across the globe. When examined from a quality perspective, design at scale relates to talent management, making sure the design function can act as an effective tactical and strategic partner for the business, and establishing effective collaboration and co-creation relationships across relevant business units and functional departments.

The need for a book dedicated to supporting design leaders was spontaneously expressed in the words of a design leader of a software company:

> Just talking to other design leaders, everybody's struggling with the same thing, pretty much: how do you integrate design into large organizations? How does design get "a seat at the table?" CDO is the new title, but that doesn't mean that design is well respected or well trusted within an organization.

These are typical questions that may arise when one is newly appointed as the executive design leader of a large complex organization. Additional, potentially overwhelming questions include the following:

- What is the commitment of the organization and its expectations about design?
- What enabling conditions are in place for design to deliver according to expectations?
- What are the key company strategies, and how can design be best aligned?
- Is the design function clearly established within the organizational structure?
- What is the overall investment in design as a function, and is this sufficient?
- How large is the actual global design organization, and how is it managed?
- What is the quality and diversity of design talent in the global team?

- What parts of the organization have already established relationships with design?
- How should the organization monitor the progress of design and its value in line with the company's ambitions?
- What short-term actions are needed to position design successfully?

To guide design leaders seeking answers to these and other kinds of questions, Figure 1.1 visualizes the Leadership for Design Excellence Model, which illustrates how to establish design excellence based on effective design leadership. The term *design excellence* refers to the preferred state of the design function, in line with its desired scope as defined in the design direction and within the organizational context — including companies' ambitions and strategic priorities. It describes a state-of-the-art design function that is fully embedded across the global organization (across functions, businesses, and regions) and is successful in maximizing its value and in driving the generation of new value for companies through growth, efficiencies, and competitive advantage.

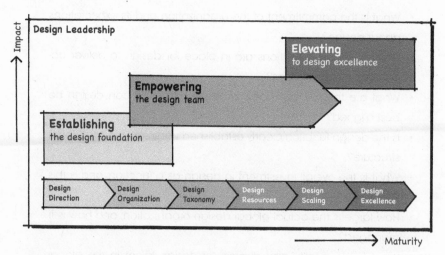

FIGURE 1.1. The Leadership for Design Excellence Model: Phases and building blocks towards design excellence at scale.

The model illustrates the idea that to create design excellence, and thereby enhance design impact and maturity, three phases are needed. These three phases are sequential, yet also somewhat overlapping:

Phase 1: Establishing the Design Foundation
Phase 2: Empowering the Design Team
Phase 3: Elevating to Design Excellence

Establishing the design foundation means setting the direction(s) that design will pursue and its rules of engagement with the rest of the organization to form a strong foundation for successful scaling of the design function. Inappropriate and ill- or undefined starting points can become distractions along the way towards design excellence.

Empowering the design team describes how to define the design function in terms of competencies, roles, and outcomes, including how to lead a design team and attract the best talent for it. Implementing this phase overlaps with the two other phases — it is a crucial, "always ongoing" phase as it is all about activities that help designers thrive at specific times, and over time.

Elevating to design excellence relates to approaches and tactics to scale a design function successfully to its preferred state. This phase can be intense and extremely complex in the context of a global matrix organization with multiple stakeholders. To achieve design excellence is already an accomplishment, but maintaining a best-in-class position over time in highly changeable business and market environments must be an ongoing pursuit.

As the model shows, design leaders will have to be patient and resilient because the journey to design excellence at scale comes with a long-term commitment and tends to be a marathon, rather than a sprint.[4] The appropriate design leadership is required to navigate and complete all three phases of the journey and is therefore the first building block towards design excellence. The figure also visualizes the other "building blocks" that feed into the three different phases. These different building blocks relate to knowledge and activities centered on certain topics needed for effective design leadership, such as design direction for defining a shared purpose;

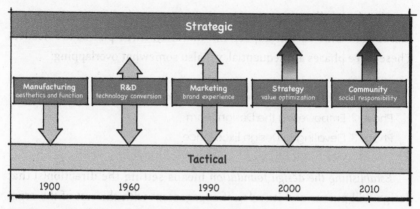

FIGURE 1.2. Evolution of the role and value of design.

design organization to create alignment on the rules for engagement; design taxonomy to define the design roles, competencies, and responsibilities; design resources to successfully lead the design team and attract the best talent; design scaling to increase the value and impact of design; and finally design excellence, being the preferred state of design at scale.

THE EVOLVING ROLE OF DESIGN

Over the last several decades, design has evolved rapidly in numerous ways. Design started around a century ago, during the 1920s, with the German Art School, the Bauhaus, which was famous for its approach to design, combining "form and function" unifying aesthetics and mass production, and which grounded the foundation for design today.[5] The scope of design and its activity has widened and deepened over time, and the nature of both its collaborations and its partners has changed substantially. It also involves a greater number of skills and competencies, and a greater variety of them, to create more and different types of value. Overall, design challenges have increased in complexity. Figure 1.2 illustrates this evolution, and highlights a shift in the focus of design away from manufacturing and towards communities.[6]

The common denominator across every stage in this shift remains the centrality of creating value for people. This used to mean, for example, designing products that were both beautiful and easier to make, and working with R&D to apply new technologies. Then the focus of design advanced into enhancing the brand experiences associated with solutions designed, which created a stronger bridge between design and marketing.[7] Design then became involved with value optimization, which led to closer alignment with the strategy function.[8] More recently, there has been a prominent shift towards creating value for communities, with a focus on sustainability, equality, and social impact.[9] Companies are taking ownership of the pathways towards a sustainable future for all.[10] "Creating value for people" no longer means only for shareholders; it encompasses a broader set of stakeholders, including customers, employees, business partners, and wider communities. Design, with its unique competencies and approaches, is well positioned to support organizations working towards this future. Design can be utilized to illustrate the meanings inherent in these shifts. It can help organizations articulate the touchpoints relevant to its key stakeholders, and help these touchpoints to manifest in engaging and relevant ways.

Figure 1.2 shows how the role and value of design has developed over time from tactical to strategic, depending on the scope of the design opportunity. This shift from tactical to strategic became especially apparent after the year 2000.[11]

TABLE 1.1. Characteristics of "design as a tactic" versus "design as a strategy."

	Design as a Tactic	Design as a Strategy
Design focus	Cost management	Value creation
Design scope	Stylistic design (afterthought)	Systematic design (front-end collaboration)
Design approach	Project-by-project (ad hoc solutions)	Portfolio approach (ecosystem solutions)
Decision making	Expertise-based (personal opinion)	Research-based (customer insights)
Design impact	Short term (quick turnaround)	Long term (master plan approach)
Delivery mechanism	Outsourcing (focus: mainstream activities)	Insourcing (focus: upstream activities)
IP potential	Mainstream repetitive activities (low potential IP space)	New breakthrough activities (high potential IP space)
Market outcomes	Fragmented market presence (portfolio confusion)	Holistic value propositions (aligned offerings)

The degree to which design is involved on a tactical or strategic level will define its added value and impact. Design leaders must be able to distinguish between requests for design that are tactical and those that are strategic. Table 1.1 lists these characteristics, and the outcomes that can be expected depending on the approach. Sharing this overview with the main stakeholders in the organization will help the design leader clarify the consequences of different approaches, manage stakeholders' expectations, and increase the general awareness inside the organization about how to utilize design best. When design is applied as a strategy, the design function focuses on value creation through front-end collaboration, resulting in a portfolio approach under which project decisions are based on customer insights. When design is applied tactically, the focus is on cost management. In this case, project decisions tend to be made ad hoc, on the basis of the personal opinions of the leaders involved, and design is often used as an afterthought, for stylistic reasons.

Ultimately, what falls within the remit of the in-house design function is context dependent. Following are examples of value areas of responsibility as mentioned by the design leaders interviewed:

- *Design for innovation*: idea generation and concepts for new value
- *Design for brand*: brand experiences designed across all customer touchpoints
- *Design for marketing*: marketing communication and storytelling for commercialization of value
- *Design for efficiency*: design smarter to drive economies-of-scale operational excellence
- *Design for customer engagement*: collaboration, co-creation, and partnership opportunities
- *Design for strategy*: exploring future scenarios based on socio-cultural and technology trends

Some of these areas of responsibility might be shared with other functions, such as marketing (branding) or R&D (innovation). Furthermore, what falls within the remit of design may change over time as the organization realigns itself with emerging design practices (such as digital design) or with redefinitions of scope initiated by the executive design leader. Chapter 5, "Design Taxonomy," will go into more depth about defining the scope of design.

While the specific scope of design will differ per organization, there is an increasing recognition that involving design as a strategic partner may bring considerable benefit to the company and its stakeholders. A greater appreciation of the ways designers work has resulted in the development and provision of internal design thinking programs, in which nondesign staff members are exposed to designers' modes of thought and action.[12] Design thinking training can enable employees companywide to adopt a more creative mindset. Creativity is not solely owned by the design function; ideally, you strive for creativity across all functions.[13] Fostering a design thinking mindset across an organization can create a better understanding and appreciation for the value that designers bring and for their work practices. This, in turn, facilitates collaboration between designers and their colleagues from other functions and business units. And because co-creation is an important component of design thinking, businesses gain a powerful way of engaging with customers, be they B2B or B2C, and identifying problem and solution spaces together.

This book is focused on elevating design at scale — building and growing the design function for scale and impact within an organization — not on how organizations can effectively develop and implement design-inspired problem-solving approaches like design thinking. Such approaches may, of course, be elements facilitating this aim, since they enable creative collaboration and co-creation across disciplines and stakeholders.

THE VALUE OF DESIGN

Companies invest in design to drive business performance and gain sustainable competitive advantage. But how does design actually contribute to business performance? Since the early 1990s, business academics have been doing research to answer this very question. Industry associations and consultancy firms have also entered the fray to deliver their insights on the value of design for the corporate world. What follows now is a brief and certainly nonexhaustive overview of some of these findings.

Several studies have focused on the influence design has on certain dimensions of a product and the subsequent impact on business results. This research suggests, for example, that through investment in design, a product's visual appearance, functionality, and ease of use can be substantially improved. As a result, consumers are more inclined to purchase the product and are also more loyal. Furthermore, good design helps to build strong brands, which, in turn, positively influences consumer buying behavior.[14]

There is also some contemporary research seeking to measure how design thinking, as a creative problem-solving approach inspired by how designers think and act, can influence product or project outcomes. Often, this research takes the form of case studies in which design thinking has been successfully applied.[15] Research measuring the impact of design thinking in a more large-scale, quantitative manner is, as yet, in limited supply. This is partly due to the fact that the design thinking approach comprises an array of tools, techniques, and processes that reveal user needs, visualize (approaches to) solutions, test and iterate on ideas, and co-create outcomes with users. Given this complexity, it is difficult to measure how it contributes to a particular outcome.[16] One example is research conducted by a consultancy firm on IBM's Enterprise Design Thinking program suggesting that applying design thinking tools and techniques results in, among other things, enhanced efficiency and speed to market, ultimately increasing profitability.[17]

Some academic studies have pursued a different avenue, examining the impact of design on an organization overall rather than at the product or project level. There is evidence that companies that invest considerable resources in design have better financial performance than companies that do not. These studies suggest that investing in good design leads to higher profit margins, among other things, which may be the result of well-designed products commanding higher premium prices than competitors' products and/or the bottom line benefitting from a more efficient manufacturing process.[18]

Research findings also indicate, however, that the impact of design on company performance is not unconditional — it is dependent on contextual factors. One important factor is the presence of effective design leadership. For example, implementing a design strategy focused on the introduction of products that are truly different from competing offerings has a particularly strong influence on final outcomes.[19] Other research suggests that when designers are included in the entire product innovation process, rather than only in one or a few phases, innovation outcomes will be enhanced.[20] Related research conducted by professional design associations suggests that companies with a systematic and comprehensive approach to design tend to outperform competitors who do not on the stock market.[21]

Interestingly, the more that design is integrated into company processes, as a strategy, the harder it seems to actually measure its sole impact. It is increasingly becoming evident, both in the literature and in practice, that successful outcomes (especially in terms of innovation and branding) depend on creative collaborations among members of multifunctional teams. Trying to filter out and determine the contribution made by a single discipline (such as design) is not only hard, it also seems counterproductive if the ultimate purpose is to create the best outcome possible together. Indeed, companies often spend a lot of time and money and effort trying to measure added value per function, and then make the (business) case for who is most successful doing so: design, marketing, R&D, whoever. This often leads to functions explaining to other functions how successful their particular contributions are, which is a suboptimal use of company resources at best. The incentive for such efforts is typically better access to company investment during its annual strategic planning cycles. But comparing functional performance, however, does not really do much to enable the kinds of collaboration across functions upon which today's successful outcomes depend.

Little attention has been paid to the value created by design beyond the purely financial, and yet it can provide strategic value, collaborative value, inspirational value, competitive value, transformational value ... the list goes on. These are areas in which design is creating intrinsic value for the organization tailored to its customer focus, collaborative approaches, creativity, and imagination. When design is embedded appropriately across the organization as a strategic function the value created by design can be more than sufficient to make design a self-funding model. That means the value created by design is substantially larger than the investments needed to support the design function. Sounds like a pretty strong business case, and points to an interesting question. Did Steve Jobs ever challenge Jony Ive about the value of design?

STRUCTURE OF THE BOOK

This book is written to support and guide design leaders as they establish, empower, and elevate creativity and design within relatively large, complex organizations. It is structured according to the three phases introduced earlier that are essential for design leaders to foster design excellence (see Figure 1.1):

Phase 1: Establishing the Design Foundation
Phase 2: Empowering the Design Team
Phase 3: Elevating to Design Excellence

The following chapters further elaborate on these phases and their constituent building blocks. Each chapter will present frameworks, tools, and best practices drawn from different organizational settings and based on insights from interviews with numerous design leaders. Each chapter also devotes attention to describing relevant challenges and dualities, and includes suggestions on how to manage these.

The journey to design excellence starts with Chapter 2, "Design Leadership." It describes the experience, tasks, and competencies an executive design leader will use to establish, navigate, and steer design from foundation to excellence at scale.

The rest of the book chapters are devoted to the other building blocks that, together, enable the design leader to elevate design at scale throughout the organization.

Phase 1: Establishing the Design Foundation

This first part of the book focuses on the knowledge and activities that together form the foundation of an effective in-house design function.

Chapter 3, "Design Direction," specifies how to formulate and implement a pathway for design that expresses the vision, mission, and principles in line with the organization's overarching strategy.

Chapter 4, "Design Organization," explains various approaches to governing the design function in terms of sponsoring, reporting lines, and staff localization.

Phase 2: Empowering the Design Team

The second part of the book describes how to build a design team and lay down the conditions that will enable the design function to flourish.

Chapter 5, "Design Taxonomy," illustrates how to classify and structure design roles and competencies according to a clear and formalized description of the design function.

Chapter 6, "Design Resources," elaborates on how to manage a world-class design team by attracting, developing, and maintaining design talent.

Phase 3: Elevating to Design Excellence

The third part of the book addresses various means of effectively scaling the design function across an organization and enabling best-in-class practices for business and community impact.

Chapter 7, "Design Scaling," details how to quantitatively and qualitatively expand design into and across multiple businesses, functions, and geographies, and explores the different engagement approaches that lead to successful design at organizationwide scale.

The final chapter, Chapter 8, "Design Excellence," brings it all together by providing industry-proven insights into what design excellence is and how to strive for it, so that in the longer term, the organization becomes best in class for design impact, and remains so.

Effective design leadership is challenging yet gratifying. During the course of this research, it was remarkable to experience the tireless efforts and limitless passion invested by design leaders to drive the development of their design functions, each in their own way. The coming chapters reveal the complex challenges and dualities that these design leaders have contended with, including some very valuable takeaways that will certainly inspire and guide effective design leadership. The ultimate aim of the book is to foster design leaders' understanding of and openness to the complexity of design leadership so that they are no longer distracted by complex challenges, nor hampered by them — they are able to contend with them in ways that build bridges toward greater benefit for all by design.

CHAPTER 2

Design Leadership

As a design leader you have the privilege of working across a diversity of cultures, organizations, and disciplines requiring sensibilities to propel meaningful collaborations.

BEING AN EXECUTIVE DESIGN LEADER is an exciting role: design is represented at the executive management level and is in a position to influence strategic directions.[1] On the other hand, that remit comes with great responsibility and the challenge of harmonizing often conflicting imperatives. To offer an example, one of these challenges is exploring new design avenues that might support company growth in the long term, while also exploiting compelling design paths that lead to results in the short term. Because the role of an executive design leader is relatively new, it is still somewhat undefined is what this senior leadership role actually entails in terms of experience, responsibilities, and the competencies needed to successfully fulfill its mission. This chapter sheds light on the matter, to show what is generally expected of an executive design leader in terms of

- background and experience;
- tasks and activities;
- competencies.

At the end of this chapter, there is a sample job description for a chief design officer. This job description captures the essence of the activities, attributes, and experience needed to be an effective executive design leader within a large complex organization. The chapter ends with an overview of some essential dualities when one is engaged in design leadership.

BACKGROUND AND EXPERIENCE OF AN EXECUTIVE DESIGN LEADER

It is important for designers wanting to become executive design leaders to know what types of background and experience might be instrumental to their career trajectory toward this role. Speaking with executive design leaders across regions and industries, studying their professional profiles, and examining recent job advertisements gave insight into what types of education and experience are specifically beneficial.

It became apparent that having a college degree in design is of real benefit. However, which design degree and specialism are relevant will depend on the type of organization and the scope of the particular design leadership role. An executive design leader working for a marketing-driven company will particularly benefit from a background in graphic design and branding; an executive design leader in a service organization will benefit from a background in digital or customer experience design; and an executive design leader working for an engineering- or technology-oriented company is particularly well-served by an education in industrial or engineering design.

Even more so than having relevant design education, executive design leaders must have extensive hands-on experience in the craft of design. As noted by a general manager of design from a professional services company, "Coming from the design craft gives you the ability to speak with authority." Interestingly, even though having hands-on experience in design is considered of utmost importance, the professionals interviewed for this book are themselves hardly ever involved anymore in hands-on design activities, given their level of seniority. However, coming from the craft of design helps establish credibility, above all from the design team. The head of design at a software company, who did not have a traditional design education background but learned the craft by doing, summed it up as follows:

> I think you have to have done hands-on design at some point in your career. I do believe that to be an effective design leader, you have to understand what it takes to go through that design process as an actual, individual contributor. It's going to be much more difficult to gain trust and credibility with your team if you have literally never done what they're doing, day to day.

While it is possible, of course, to gather knowledge about the design process and the appropriate design tools and methods by studying relevant publications or by being exposed to design activities, it is more difficult to steer and guide designers when not having been immersed in the design craft in the past. For example, when design leaders were asked to indicate who they admired as a design leader and why, their appreciation tended to be partly based on the hard skills of these so-called "design virtuosos." One VP of design at a company operating within the DIY industry described another design leader in this way:

> He had all the design skills and all the passion. He had excellent skills. He would draw, sketch, come up with ideas. We were designers, didn't know too much — just working passionately on design. He could speak in a much more comprehensive vein, developing the future, developing tools, future opportunities . . . very highly respected for that. Hard design skills are one of the things I always admire.

Next to an education and a good deal of practical design experience, many design leaders interviewed also indicated that it was of great benefit to have received some type of business education (like an MBA) and/or experience in more business-related roles. This greatly facilitates the interaction across functions and management levels within the organization, because the design leader can "speak their language." For example, a VP of design from a pharmaceutical company had not only worked in design but had also held positions inside other functions, including marketing and business development:

> Thanks to my background, I can talk to a lot of different functions in an organization and sound quite credible, because I'm not a purist with twenty-five years in design. It also means I'm quite pragmatic and bottom-line when it comes to doing my job.

Overall, an effective executive design leader is someone who has a dual background. They can operate in a world driven by creativity and the exploration of "what could be," and they can operate in a world driven by business and exploitation of "what is." What's more, they are able to switch between these worlds with agility.

TASKS AND ACTIVITIES OF THE EXECUTIVE DESIGN LEADER

Within the literature, management is often juxtaposed with leadership.[2] Leadership tends to be described in terms of setting a future direction and inspiring people to embrace this direction and help achieve it. Management is described in terms of planning, making sure day-to-day activities are happening as they should and goals are actually achieved, giving directions. In reality, executive design leadership includes both leadership and management-related activities.

Furthermore, an executive design leader's job will depend on how highly the company prioritizes design as a driver of value and competitive advantage. For example, in technology-driven B2B companies, design might be expected to advance the company's innovation efforts, but in marketing-driven B2C companies, design may carry more weight in terms of branding and customer experience. However, despite the scope of this range, it is still possible to identify core design leadership tasks. They can be divided into three categories:

- Strategy (direction setting)
- Communications (stakeholder engagement)
- Organization (building structure and driving culture)

In the following subsections, each of these categories and the tasks associated with them are briefly described.[3]

Strategy

One of the core tasks of executive design leaders is to engage in strategy work. They must guide the design team and help the company reach its objectives. Strategy work includes establishing a design vision and mission, formulating and implementing design principles and values, and defining long(er)-term design strategies and roadmaps to implement them. By means of their strategic work, executive design leaders guide and inspire the design team. They orient them in the direction design will go, like a lighthouse, and provide them with a purpose that extends well into the long term, also demonstrating how everyone's work is serving and achieving the overarching ambitions of the organization.

An example of a strategic direction provided to the design team can be found in GE Healthcare. This organization formulated a design philosophy labeled "The Magic of Science and Empathy," suggesting that GE Healthcare designers enrich user experiences "with technology, delight, hope, and an understanding of human needs." The design values that undergird this philosophy include "authenticity; empathic design; shared intelligence and trusted relationships; imagination at work; essential expression and the science and mathematics of beauty."[4]

Next to articulating the strategic direction, design leaders should also make sure this strategic direction is actually understood and implemented by their design team. The VP of design at a company operating in the automotive industry described the following approach for communicating and implementing a specific strategic direction:

I say, "We're going to reach that mountain top," and then I have to make sure that my design directors understand *which* mountain top they are going to climb. In terms of how they climb it and which path they take, that is basically up to them to figure out. But then, in between, I would guide them to make sure they are not veering off course. They all should have a common understanding of where they need to go.

In Chapter 3, "Design Direction," we will further discuss how to engage in design strategy work.

Communications

Another core task of executive design leadership is leveraging several communication activities inside and outside the organization. The aim of these activities will be to position the design function, educate stakeholders about design and its scope, and share best practices that inspire and demonstrate the impact design could have.

External Communications

Executive design leaders should be design champions and thought leaders, and not only within the organization but also in the wider world. This can be achieved by delivering keynote speeches at conferences; writing blogs, articles for professional magazines, and posts on LinkedIn; doing podcasts; or giving interviews with the media. Media exposure is correlated with one's reputation as thought leader — someone recognized as an authority in their field, pioneering new ideas that will move the profession forward.

There are different benefits stemming from design leaders sharing their insights and knowledge with the outside world:

- It attracts and inspires design talent.
- It contributes to and furthers the public conversation about design.
- It enables dialogue with and learning from other design leaders outside the organization.
- It helps establish and reinforce the positioning of the design function within the organization.
- It explains to new and existing customers what design can bring.

While many of the design leaders interviewed for this book do communicate about their activities publicly, some valid concerns were raised. Overall, a careful balance must be kept between the amount of time design leaders devote to their leadership tasks and the amount they spend on external communication activities — assuming external engagement is not their main task. Following are some other checks and balances for external communication:

- External communication activities are performed, above all, for the greater good of the organization and the design team. Thus, the first question design leaders should ask themselves when deciding on an external communication engagement is, "How is this communication activity advantageous from an organizational standpoint?" There is a thin line between engaging in thought leadership to benefit the organization and doing so for personal prestige.

- External communication activities such as keynote speeches and lectures can motivate, bringing energy and confidence to those engaged in them. As a result, external communication should not only be the responsibility of the executive design leader but should also be a task — or opportunity — allocated to other members of the design leadership team to help advance their thought leadership and positioning as inspirational and respected design professionals.

- For effective external communication, the design leader should be open to active input and support from internal and external communications professionals and PR specialists. Formal media training is a good way of developing effective external communications skills and learning to interact with confidence with journalists and reporters across different media (broadcast, print, digital, and social).

- The design leader should carefully consider what knowledge to share with the outside world. Some knowledge is sensitive or confidential because of the competitive edge it provides and should then not be shared, of course.

- Design leaders should share authentic, credible, impactful, and inspirational stories with their audiences. For example, if the organization is still on the path to being truly design-led, then a story about how to further develop and promote design culture may be more appropriate and credible than a story on accomplished design excellence.

- If it so happens that the organization frequently hosts various external design and business audiences (partners, academia, or customers, for example) it may be worthwhile to invest in a dedicated design space that allows for effective hosting of events.

Internal Communications

Internal communications include design team communications and exchanges with other internal functions and organizational stakeholders.

Design Team Communications

A design leader's communications with the design team include the diffusion of information about strategy, including company and design strategies, and core design principles guiding design team activities, behaviors, and mindsets.

In order to effectively disseminate strategy-related knowledge, a design leader must translate overarching company strategies in a way that that will allow the design team to understand how it will impact their jobs — why there will be a strategic move in a particular direction, for example — so they can better understand, relate to, and align their efforts with this strategy. For example, if digital transformation is a company strategy, leaders need to be able to explain why that change is important, how it will affect designers' practice, and how the transformation is to be embedded in design activities and outcomes. A VP of design from a toy company noted the following regarding a main responsibility towards the design team:

I explain the strategy in a way that makes sense for my creative leads, so they have the framework they need to get on with their jobs. When I have dialogues with them, my job is not to say whether something should be red or blue. It's to say, "Does this fit the strategy? Is there something else we could be doing that would be a better fit?"

Chapter 6, "Design Resources," provides more detail on communication with design teams.

Communications with Nondesign Stakeholders

Every design leader performs the important role of championing design within the organization. Educating other functional, business, and regional teams about what the design team has to offer and how to effectively collaborate with the design team is a large part of this. Indeed, continually educating organizational stakeholders about design tends to take up a substantial amount of many design leaders' time, particularly when design is an emerging function and relatively new to the organization.[5] For example, in a prior publication,[6] Eric pointed out,

> I am continuously educating the organization about design, upward and downward. If people don't have appreciation for design, is it because they don't appreciate design? Or because they don't know what design is about? I give as much internal keynotes as external keynotes to make sure we are connecting and explaining our role well.

To explain what design is contributing in comparison with other organizational functions, the design leaders interviewed often refer to their unique, human-centered approach, discovering and representing the (latent) needs of customers and users. This sometimes results in tensions with marketing — a discipline that also provides insights about markets and customer needs and wishes.[7] A way to resolve this tension is to engage in effective stakeholder management and build and foster collaborative relationships with marketing. Indeed, the design leaders we interviewed revealed a number of different approaches for effectively educating and engaging with organizational stakeholders at every level about what design does and the value it offers.

- *Storytelling*: Design leaders share stories about customer or user experiences to illustrate how products and services are impacting and should impact customers' lives. Effective storytelling helps draw the audience in, emotionally.

- *Targeting messages*: Design leaders adjust the language of their stories somewhat depending on the audience. When speaking with senior executives, for example, the language becomes more business-centric and data driven, because "that is vocabulary that senior management relate to," according to the global head of design at a fast-moving consumer goods company.

- *Sharing case studies*: Design leaders compile and share case studies describing the successful projects carried out by their design teams to demonstrate the effectiveness and impact of design. They speak not only in terms of design outcomes (such as improved user experiences), but also in terms of improving overall business results.

- *Making design understandable*: Design leaders bring clarity to what their designers do, by discussing ongoing projects and specifying and aligning on the activities (best) done by designers versus those (best) done by other functions. Providing transparency about what designers do, and how they do it, helps to erase the perception that design is a kind of black box, or that designers are "magicians in black shirts" (head of design, telecommunications company).

- *Offering design workshops*: Design leaders and their teams engage in codesign workshops, design immersions, and design sprints alongside colleagues working inside other organizational functions, for example to jointly identify and prioritize emerging market trends to be explored. Immersing others in the world of design fosters greater practical understanding about how designers work day to day and may also result in increased engagement and commitment towards the outcomes of these workshops.

- *Creating a display area*: Design leaders establish and maintain a space dedicated to exhibiting design achievements. This area preferably is available to all inside the organization, and potentially also external audiences, to showcase successful design projects completed and possible future design concepts (for example, visualized future scenarios).

Chapter 7, "Design Scaling," further illustrates how the approaches above can act as catalysts for deeper commitment to and investment in design.

Organization

Next to strategy and communication, another core task of the executive design leader is to lead the design function within the overall organization. They are responsible for the establishment and implementation of effective design processes, procedures, and frameworks that will structure the design function. More in-depth information on how to define and implement effective governance and taxonomy frameworks for the design function is provided later in the book.

Many of the design leaders interviewed for this book stressed that running the design function includes creating an environment in which designers can work effectively and productively, in which they can flourish. They do this by paving the way for creativity and design. The head of design at a professional services company described the importance of providing "oxygen" for the design team:

> Chief design officers . . . spend much of their time creating breathing space for designers to thrive. Because organizations are often focused on optimization, efficiency, replicability, and consistency, and also on lowering costs and avoiding risk, it is challenging for design to survive. It's almost like getting covered by a blanket and you're constantly trying to push it off by showing proof and results, bringing people along, communicating, showing commitment . . . getting things out of the way for your design team to actually empower them to deliver great results.

Providing oxygen for the design team to flourish and be creative is an essential task of the executive design leader. As described by the senior VP of design at a process transformation company, this task is akin to creating a "creative bubble" for the design team: an environment in which the designers' needs are met and they can focus on their creativity. This is not necessarily an easy task, but it is essential. "What is really important is to shield my designers from the 'corporate machine.' This is crucial for their happiness, not necessarily mine. I have the 'stress and the ulcers' — but that's my job, right?"

Creating breathing space for design also includes activities that will guide the overarching organizational culture towards being more design driven. This imperative might come in the form of an explicit corporate assignment or could be the design leader's professional ambition. To help create a more design-driven organizational culture, the design leader interviewees once again pointed to the importance of effective internal positioning and education about design. The director of design at a software development and services company stated that, ultimately, what is needed is to build "a culture where everybody cares about good design, not just me and my designers."

Another core organizational task of the executive design leader is to coordinate and align the design function with the other functions in the organization and with other executives. Core organizational functions that tend to work together with design are strategy, marketing and branding, and R&D. An executive design leader needs to engage in horizontal coordination efforts with these functions to establish internal alignment on priorities, strategies, and programs. This can be done by making sure there is "a constant flow of information and dialogue between the different functions," according to the CDO of a PC hardware peripherals company. Because each function has its own focus and priorities, and these can sometimes be conflicting, ensuring internal alignment and acting as an emissary for design are both necessary parts of the executive design leader's role.

Internal alignment naturally includes engaging in activities that support the CEO's overall agenda. For example, when making decisions about design projects, the executive design leader should prioritize projects that directly contribute to fulfilling the organization's stated strategic priorities. Reaching strategic targets means project prioritization, which also implies candid discussions about what projects to discontinue, or reprioritize, both within the design team and among executive peers. These discussions end up serving wider strategic planning activities, such as the organization's (annual) strategic planning sessions and budgeting cycle reviews. The executive design leader has to ensure that the design team has the resources it needs to support the company strategies properly.

Finally, another core organizational task for the executive design leader is being responsible for monitoring, control, and compliance. This may entail the development of a "scorecard" to assess design performance and establish metrics that will contribute to assessing progress and value creation. Even if organizational leadership demands it, isolating and assessing design's impact on outcomes and value creation is challenging. Once the relevant financial and nonfinancial performance indicators have been determined, in collaboration and aligned with the Executive Board, the executive design leader is subsequently responsible to track progress and take corrective actions when targets are not met. More on the "how" of monitoring and control can be found in Chapter 3, "Design Direction."

Exhibit 2.1 presents the schedule of activities in a typical week of Eric in his executive design leadership role. It gives a flavor of the breadth and depth of what design leaders' engagement could be.

COMPETENCIES OF THE EXECUTIVE DESIGN LEADER

Executive design leaders must acquire specific competencies to execute their role effectively. These competencies overlap, in part, with those required by senior executives in general. Here we focus on those that are more specific to executive design leaders, including some specific ways that generic leadership attributes can be brought to life by design leaders. These are the capacity to

- bridge the worlds of design and business;
- master stakeholder management;
- instigate change for progress;
- inspire and lead by example;
- be a proactive intrapreneur.

The coming sections treat each of these in detail.

Weekdays	Week Schedule
Monday	**Meeting with brand design team and engineering colleagues:** review a new corporate branding initiative to establish and implement an appropriate set of standards and guidelines for the company's interior design. Get stakeholders' feedback about the guidelines and begin to plan out communications and implementation approaches.
	New employee orientation meeting: share company strategies, relevant design developments and approaches including the roadmap going forward. Roundtable: elaborate on the strategic nature of design.
	Lunch meeting with local nonprofit organization: explore ways to amplify existing collaborations, keep momentum going, and raise new funds using the relationships with the company and the design team.
	Session with high potential business leader: mentor a mentee as part of the company leadership development program. Topic of discussion: transformation and change in a world of Six Sigma. Open question to explore from last session: how to be a change agent by doing more of the same (better)?
Tuesday	**Leadership team meeting:** conduct operational review with global design leaders and discussion about diversity and inclusion of how design can lead by example. IT guest will discuss design software application management and ways to line up IT interests with design, and vice versa.
	Update with the global communications leader: review ongoing communications projects and potential new opportunities. Discuss any speeches or interviews requested and scheduled, or any other relevant events to position design (internal or external).
Wednesday	**Breakfast HQ design team meeting:** have several design teams share project (interim) outcomes and best practices. New hire introductions. Deliver news regarding important upcoming internal company and design team initiatives.
	Attend a UX design team masterclass on the Internet of Things: comment on the ideas generated by smaller cross-company working groups (in a dragon's den with two other business colleagues).

(continues)

Weekdays	Week Schedule
	Meet the leader of the design prototype lab: discuss expansion of the space and investment needed for new rapid prototyping equipment. Next steps: investment sign off, green light from engineering to modify the space.
Thursday	**Meet with branding team and the ad agency:** review the creative work for a new brand campaign and its media plan. Prepare next steps: executive board meeting to introduce the campaign approach and agreement on annual investments requested.
	Partnership update meeting with premium branded company: discuss joined development activities and related marketing planning of joined product introductions. Creative concepts are reviewed by both parties and prepared for commercialization. Great co-branding opportunity based on the strengths of two reputable brands.
	Monthly update with business group design leader: discuss design team operations and update on the realization of additional design studio as part of new company R&D center of excellence and agree on next steps.
Friday	**Monthly financial controller update:** review design financial monthly report and agree on items for follow up. Discuss global alignment about how to generate next level of financial reporting of the global design spent across all organizational entities.
	Call with the Asian team: discuss upcoming visit and briefing on possible events, a speaking opportunity at the local college of design, and the national leadership team's great interest in opening up a dialogue with design.
	Meeting with the CEO and other executive leaders: discuss communication and a visualization approach about updated company priorities and strategies for introduction at the upcoming investors' day. Exploration about how to simplify the messaging and some possible advanced concepts to update the narrative of the story.

EXHIBIT 2.1. Schedule of typical activities when engaged in executive design leadership.

Competency: Bridging the Worlds of Design and Business

To effectively operate in a corporate, for-profit context, executive design leaders must have business acumen and take responsibility for the business component of their work — if only to guarantee the longevity of the design team. To quote the head of design from an automotive company, "We can make beautiful cars; but if they don't sell, then investment in design will dry up soon."

Different functions have different priorities and goals, which, ultimately, should ladder up to the CEO's priorities. Often, trade-offs using available resources will need to be made to fulfill these priorities, since resources are never unlimited. It is thus important for a design leader to empathize with the broader business context rather than "trying to push design for the sake of design," as the director of design at a healthcare company put it. Without knowledge and sensitivity towards diverging priorities, goals, and resource limitations, it may be very hard to "manage design ideas through the organization," according to the design director at a consumer packaged goods company. Indeed, many have recognized how difficult it is to implement new ideas in large organizations. Inside the "design powerhouse" that is Samsung Electronics, here is how the challenge is described:

> In large companies, the process of innovation is long and tortuous. Even if a design team's new product concept wins raves and garners executive support, it still must survive numerous downstream decisions — by engineers, programmers, user-experience experts, team leaders, managers, and even, in some cases, suppliers. Each of those decisions creates an opportunity for an idea to be hijacked by other functions' priorities and the strong tendency to steer the process toward the safety of incremental change rather than the risky territory of radical innovation.[8]

Design leaders should not only be able to create and identify great ideas that are likely to result in business growth — they must also be able to guide these ideas through the organizational system until they are actually successfully commercialized.

The need to be business savvy does not mean the design leader has to be a seasoned business leader, necessarily. The executive design leader and their design team are of value to the organization because they bring a different perspective. A careful balance between being business-like versus being design-like is essential to secure design integrity. As the head of design at an automotive company so rightly said, "A design leader needs to have one foot in creativity and one foot in business."

Executive design leaders must not only be aware of business-related goals and priorities and take these into account during decision making or internal alignment. They must also translate business decisions into context for design teams, to keep them informed and clarify the business perspective they will be working with. The design leader needs to be transparent, ultimately, about the design results that are to be met. One of the design leaders interviewed shared that designers sometimes can be slightly idealistic and forget to focus on delivering results in the short term. This particular general manager of design at a professional services company noted that design leaders must "teach designers to respect the business and teach business people to respect designers."

Competency: Mastering Stakeholder Management

For effective alignment with other functions and at every level of the organization, an executive design leader must have excellent networking skills. According to the general manager of design from a multinational healthcare company, effective networking helps to build trusting relationships in the workplace and is the most essential ingredient "for getting things done in an organization." Above all, design leaders must be able to engage with all kinds of organizational stakeholders, not only designers; ascertaining how design can collaborate (more) effectively with other functions in the organization depends on this skill. It may be helpful if design leaders can learn the language and become familiar with the way of thinking of these other functions. For example, many senior executives prefer to make decisions based on facts and figures, are sensitive to rational arguments, and prefer engagements that get straight to the point. Design leaders may want to adjust their language accordingly, if only "to build credibility for the design point of view" (global design director, PC hardware firm). Designers possess the capacity to empathize with and capture the latent needs of customers to translate into innovative solutions. If designers would use more of this empathy to connect better with colleagues from other functions, design would be much more effective and successful in the end. Indeed, empathy is considered the hallmark of twenty-first-century creative leadership.[9]

While many design leader interviewees subscribed to the idea that effective engagement with executive management or other organizational stakeholders requires adjustments in language, it may be counterproductive to fully embrace "business speak and behavior." What is needed is a careful balance between being empathetic and adjusting to business language, and being a proud designer and celebrating design language, since this is what makes designers unique and invaluable. The language of design includes qualitative arguments that capture emotional drivers and core experiences, which may include verbal or visual storytelling, and even perhaps the use of experiential demonstrators: short videos or visualizations that "help people imagine" and by means of which "people can really feel it," according to the design director at a lighting solutions company. The general manager of design working for a professional services company illustrated the benefit of mixing business and design languages when communicating with the C-suite in this way:

> The C-suite always likes numbers. And having the business case behind the design strategy that you're putting forward is indeed really powerful and necessary. But I actually think that for the C-suite, good storytelling and true conviction is also really powerful. Because, at the end of the day, they're also human.

Competency: Instigating Change for Progress

Executive design leaders should be fearless. They must be able to stand up for what they believe in. Many of the leaders interviewed stressed this. The head of design from a financial services company noted that leaders defend the design team and promote their human-centric proposals and priorities because these are "good for the company too." And another head of design from a global home appliances company recalled a prior executive design leader in their company who was "provoking" others in the C-suite, to convince them that making consumers "emotionally connect" with the company's products should be a core objective. These provocations led to friction and conflict, but ultimately contributed to "increased esteem for the design team" and helped the company reposition itself effectively.

Eric has suggested that part of his design leadership role consists of being a "corporate rebel . . . with purpose." A design leader should be a "stretch agent," pushing the organization to think about what could be and inviting it to change for the better.[10] But don't be a rebel for rebel's sake — be a rebel with a cause: to drive progress. Being a design leader is, in a way, being subversive; they stretch the notion of what could be feasible within the organization.[11] Being a rebel with a cause requires the willingness (and the capacity) "to stand up straight and champion design," and thereby ensure that design priorities and values are sufficiently considered, according to the CDO of a financial services company.

Even as design leaders challenge others, they also need to find common ground and support the organization's priorities and efforts to attain its overarching goals. This may require strategic decision making, for example in terms of design resource prioritization. To prioritize design resources implies making decisions about areas to focus on and not focus on, for example in terms of the number and scope of projects. Fulfilling the organization's goals and priorities implies "constantly trading off and leveraging design resources in a way that benefits the organization in the best way possible," says the VP of design at a global automotive parts company. One leader (the global head of design at a consumer goods company) describes the ability to prioritize design resources as "the art of saying no." This art is extended to dealings with design teams, if they want to explore a certain market opportunity that does not fit the strategic agenda of the business unit they work for, for example, or when that market opportunity has been deemed unviable or unfeasible. The art of saying no may also be used towards business colleagues, for example if they request design resources for incremental short-term activities that might be nice to have but will not have any real impact.

Competency: Inspiring and Leading by Example

For a vibrant design culture, executive design leaders should inspire their design team to deliver high-quality work (again and again) and continue to grow and learn. To this end, they can provide an inspirational design vision or mission and publish transparent design principles that guide designers' work activities.

To be inspiring, leaders must constantly keep an eye on trends and developments and adjust and redefine their leadership activities accordingly. For example, on the basis of their analysis of trends and developments, an executive design leader may formulate a vision for the organization's future and set activities in motion to make that future happen. To be successful at this, the leader must exercise design thought leadership: pioneer the fresh new ideas that will propel the design function, and the organization at large, further. For example, some years ago the head of design of a global home appliances company instigated the company's digital transformation by setting a "North Star" objective: build an in-house digital design resource. That plan included a roadmap on how to get there.

Many design leaders interviewed noticed the importance of leading by example. Effective leadership means providing inspiration to the design team and the organization at large by getting things done the best way possible. Many times over the years, Eric has emphasized and acted on the belief that good design leadership is about "showing, not telling." For example, early on in his role as CDO for 3M, Eric teamed up with the CMO and garnered executive management support to introduce a new brand platform and design an entirely new corporate visual identity system, which was implemented in 2015. This was a truly transformational and collaborative initiative that touched many points across the organization and demonstrated the impact of collaborative creativity and design within the company. It resulted in more visual cohesion and an outspoken positioning for the 3M Company brand and was accompanied by a substantial increase in brand equity over the following years, as measured by Interbrand.[12]

Competency: Being an Intrapreneur

Another important attribute of an executive design leader is being intrapreneurial and initiating new projects or activities that are not necessarily asked for or even expected. In general, an executive design leader's scope is not defined in detail, so there is room to explore interesting opportunities that present themselves along the way. Interesting intrapreneurial opportunities to pursue are usually those that assist in embedding and elevating design inside the organization. An exemplary intrapreneurial initiative is that of a head of design working for a telecommunications company, who established and implemented successful customer experience labs that brought end-to-end customer journeys to life in their entirety, and provided a physical space for everybody in the organization to interact with customers. Before this, customer experience was not being orchestrated across various organizational silos, which had been negatively affecting outcomes overall. When the design function is relatively new and the other organizational functions do not have much experience collaborating with designers, an executive design leader may have to actively seek out partners within the organization who have the appetite to participate in novel intrapreneurial projects together.

Which intrapreneurial initiative to pursue is basically the prerogative of the design leader, although it should offer value to the organization to start with. The selection is partly based on a gut feeling developed over time, in turn based on experience, of what may work or not and what is likely to be relevant.[13] Finding proof up front that the intrapreneurial initiative will be a success is hard, particularly if it relates to something that has not been done before. Such initiatives should be seen as explorative design experiments similar to experiments in R&D. Indeed, being intrapreneurial will not always deliver successful outcomes, as is the case with intrapreneurship in general. The general manager of design at a healthcare company noted the following:

> You fail at least as often as you succeed when you try to do new and interesting things that management did not ask you to do. Indeed, maybe you fail more often than you succeed, but you do it for the right reasons — with good intentions.

Even if intrapreneurial ventures fail, the leaders who initiated these for the benefit of the company at large need opportunities to experiment with and learn from these failures nevertheless. The key is to be patient and resilient: keep seeking opportunities, keep pushing for change and innovation continuously. This is particularly needed since, as noted by a head of design from a large professional services company, large organizations "tend to change ever so slowly. . . . Every day the inertia of the organization is to be faced."

THE EXECUTIVE DESIGN LEADER JOB DESCRIPTION

In Exhibit 2.2, we provide an example of a job description for a chief design officer/executive design leader who will manage and develop the design function for a large, global enterprise. This job description was assembled using information gleaned from real-world, existing job descriptions and postings for design leaders operating at a senior, executive level across a variety of companies. It summarizes the main elements discussed in this chapter.

A job description generally starts with a description of the company the executive design leader will work for and details about the organizational context (such as reporting lines, size of the design team, location). We will not provide that information in our example, given that it is a hypothetical template for any sector.

Job descriptions often list desired outcomes, which will naturally depend on the specific organization involved, and so are not included here. However, following are some examples of desired outcomes:

- Establishing design as a core capability that drives the company's growth and sustainable competitive advantage
- Elevating the position of design to a more strategic level, going beyond operational or tactical execution, helping to formulate customer-centric strategies
- Advancing and supporting outstanding, consistent customer experiences
- Creating or further reinforcing brand differentiation
- Establishing an organizational culture that fosters innovation with high-quality creative engagements

Job Description CDO/Executive Design Leader	
Our organization is searching for an executive design leader who will be responsible for leading design and creativity within the company globally and for establishing and maintaining design functional excellence. Below is a list of the key responsibilities, competencies, and qualifications that candidates must possess or be able to demonstrate.	
	Key Responsibilities
Vision and strategy	- Establishing the vision of how design will add value to the company, which includes setting forth future opportunities and new strategic directions and translating the company's' ambitions and priorities into effective design strategies and actual design programs. The vision also includes how design will impact company decision making in terms of strategic prioritization and maximizing design investments to create sustainable competitive advantage.
	- Championing design within the organization and externally; driving the growth and scaling of design within the organization (at all levels and across the whole organization); managing the organization's design reputation within the external community.
Execution	- Being an effective collaborator, connecting the dots across different organizational functions and business activities in ways that will identify opportunities to drive growth and efficiency and optimize customer experience; working closely with functional and business leaders and shaping the way design is integrated in the organization.
	- Growing the design team and advancing team expertise: developing and implementing appropriate design processes, practices, and tools that support replicable and scalable design impact; attracting, developing, training, and retaining a diverse and highly talented team of design professionals; driving and fostering an environment and culture in which design can thrive.
	- Internalizing corporate strategy and developing and communicating design strategy to ensure that the role and impact of design are understood within the broader design organizational structure; ensuring that the design team understands how to bring the corporate strategy to life with their activities.

Key competencies	– Think strategically; drive a long-term vision of design; effectively use qualitative and quantitative insights to drive strategy.
	– Challenge the status quo to improve and innovate organizational outcomes; be a proactive leader who initiates and influences aspects of the organization to drive progress.
	– Manage things through others; build high-performing, diverse creative teams composed of multiple disciplines and empower and enable them to flourish.
	– Navigate stakeholder relationships; build and foster effective networking as a way to create understanding, alignment, and momentum for design.
	– Instigate and implement new initiatives to utilize design within the organization; remain cognizant of the business realities and organizational context.
	– Inspire and mentor the design team as a whole; cultivate and promote exceptional design talent; identify and manage possible limitations to guarantee high-quality design outcomes; build a culture that attracts creative professionals.
Key qualifications	– Extensive (10+ years) experience in (global) design leadership roles; demonstrated ability to build and lead high-performing design teams.
	– Wide-ranging design experience; a career spanning a variety of design disciplines, industries, and cultures is strongly preferred.
	– Demonstrated business acumen; demonstrated ability to maximizes creativity and design in a way that supports and enhances company strategies in true partnership with other C-suite colleagues.
	– Excellent (written, verbal, and visual) communication skills; the natural ability to communicate across all levels of an organization through powerful storytelling.
	– A track record of media appearances and public design advocacy; a recognized thought leader in the global design community.
	– Bachelor's degree or higher from a design-centric field; experience representing design successfully in an enterprise business environment.

EXHIBIT 2.2. Sample job description of a chief design officer/executive design leader.

CONCLUSION

This chapter contains an overview of the background, tasks, and competencies associated with an executive design leader. As identified by the design leaders interviewed, the most prominent challenge when executing their role is maintaining a balance between design and business priorities and goals. A design leader needs to truly understand and share an affinity with business when operating in a for-profit environment and thus include aspects of viability and feasibility when making decisions. Yet the central task of a design leader is to represent and advocate for the design perspective and not turn into a business leader. To do so, what is needed from an executive design leader is the following:

- To engage in enlightened empathy;[14] be sensitive and adapt to business requirements related to viability and feasibility, but also try to stretch what is considered to be viable and feasible to get the design point of view across.
- To champion design and its ways of working while also conforming to existing business practices. This may require, for example, the provision of facts and figures that ground design proposals, and a communication style that is clear and to the point, but it may also include the use of different, design-driven practices such as inspiring storytelling (in words or visually) to bring design experiences to life.
- To steward transformation, engaging in a ceaseless effort to drive change (to stretch); be a catalyst to challenge existing paradigms but also continually seek to build bridges (create buy-in) between functions and departments to foster teamwork and collaboration that makes change possible.
- To design the future, lead with confidence, and have a vision for the way forward for design, yet still be open to other ideas, be they from the design team or from others within or outside the organization.
- To insist on creating stakeholder value, with a focus on customers while also ensuring business and community value.

Being an executive design leader is an exciting yet challenging role. This book contains many more insights to guide prospective leaders in their quest for functional and professional design excellence. The information contained in coming chapters will describe the wider landscape surrounding executive design leaders, where they will put the expertise described here to use, pioneering the way forward for design.

PART 1

Establishing the Design Foundation

CHAPTER 3

Design Direction

A thoroughly articulated design direction orients team efforts. It acts as a beacon for the design team, inspiring and guiding them to take charge of the journey ahead.

THE PATH TO DESIGN EXCELLENCE is a long and impervious one. Approaching it with a long-term perspective and a well-thought-out course of action provides a solid foundation when journeying towards design excellence. Design leaders need to actively define the direction that the design function will take, and then plan its implementation with transparency and confidence. This demands time and energy — setting a course for design includes consideration of several, equally important components that must be not only developed consistently but also iterated upon and "socialized" among members of the design team and the company at large. This is no simple task.

Figure 3.1 visualizes the different components of the design direction, which are then explained in detail in the paragraphs that follow.

The first section focuses on how to set a direction informed by a clear design vision, mission, and set of principles, with some guidelines for how to formulate each of these components. The following sections describe how to implement the design direction through the strategy, roadmap, and annual operational plan. There is also information about how executive

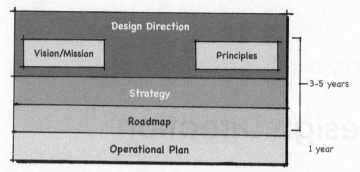

FIGURE 3.1. Components that inform the design direction.

design leaders can utilize the expertise of their teams to identify and refine the design direction components. After that, the following section introduces some guidelines on how to communicate the design direction and how to use performance metrics to monitor implementation progress. The chapter concludes with an overview of certain dualities that emerge as the contours of the design direction come into focus, and guidelines on how to deal with those.

SETTING DIRECTION: DEFINING ITS VISION, MISSION, AND PRINCIPLES

Defining a direction for the design team to pursue is a core responsibility of executive design leaders and one of the first steps they should take when following up on the mandate given by the company. Outlining a direction for the design function starts with defining the function's vision, mission, and principles.

A vision is a statement describing an inspiring and desired future for a company (or a business unit, or an organizational function).[1] A design vision is an ambitious statement that sets the course for the future, acting as a source of inspiration and motivation for the design team. According to the head of strategic design at a professional services company, "From a design leader perspective, you want to make sure that designers are being challenged, passions are being fed, and they feel like there's a purpose."

Based on the definition of an organizational mission,[2] a design mission is a clear and memorable statement describing what the design team does and why. Compared to the design vision, a design mission is more actionable, as it translates the forward-looking content of the vision into actual modes of work for the design team. Eric and his leadership team developed the following mission for the design function:

> Through collaborative creativity, we design meaningful brand experiences and enrich innovation. Our diverse design competencies help drive competitive advantage, grow our business, delight our customers, and make a positive impact on our world.[3]

This design mission establishes collaborative creativity as the way the design team will work, which includes design thinking approaches, creative workshops, and multidisciplinary teamwork with relevant stakeholders in the organization. The mission also explains what the design team does, in this case that it will be designing brand experiences and enhancing innovation efforts. Finally, the mission states explicitly how the design team will generate value for the company and society at large, which, in this case, is to support the drive towards competitive advantage, business growth, and customer satisfaction, and make a positive impact on the world.

Along with a design vision and mission, design leaders often identify design principles as an additional framework to guide their team. Design principles should reflect the design vision and offer the design team clear guidance on how to make everyday decisions (in other words, stimulate desirable behaviors) and how to practice their craft (in other words, stimulate desirable design outcomes). Design leaders formulate design principles in different ways. Some focus more on design outcomes and the design processes leading to them. This is the case at Salesforce, a provider of enterprise cloud software, which specified four design principles that, it says, everybody should "keep in mind when making design decisions"[4]:

- *Clarity:* Ambiguity should be eliminated; people should be able to see, understand, and act with confidence.
- *Efficiency:* Workflows should be streamlined and optimized; needs should be anticipated to help people work better, smarter, and faster.
- *Consistency:* Familiarity should be created and intuition strengthened by applying the same solution to the same problem.

- *Beauty:* People's time and attention should be respected through thoughtful and elegant craftsmanship.

Other design leaders prefer formulations that focus on designers' general behaviors beyond the design process, when, for instance, they collaborate with other functions or take over leadership tasks. Given this remit, certain design leaders prefer the label "design values" to "design principles," although in general these two labels seem to be used interchangeably. For instance, the CDO of a financial services company created the following list of design values to guide the general behavior of the design team:

- *Clarity,* which refers to addressing the complexity of financial information
- *Compassion,* which refers to deeper understanding about what makes the life of people better
- *Connection,* which refers to acting collaboratively within and outside the team
- *Courage,* which refers to daring to go for the most innovative path
- *Craft,* which refers to pursuing high-quality design standards

Design principles, regardless of their formulation, should guide designers without constraining their creativity and assist them in creating outcomes that fulfill the goals of both the design function and the company as a whole. Design principles form the foundation of the design culture (to be) established within the organization. Formulating and internalizing these principles allows the design team to truly own and live by them.

ENHANCING THE DIRECTION: SOME GUIDELINES

When setting a future direction for the design function — be it a vision, a mission, or a set of principles — there are several aspects that the design leader should take into account.

Content

The direction should combine information on the scope of design with inspirational components aimed at engaging current and future design team members and other key stakeholders. As suggested by prior research,[5] well-conceived visions or missions should balance core ideology (describing the core values, scope, and purpose of the company) with the envisioned future (describing the future goal in a vivid and inspiring manner). The mission of Philips Design offers a good example of how these two elements are balanced. "We bring human-centered innovation to the technologies we all rely on for healthcare and healthy living. The products, services, and solutions we design touch the lives of millions every day. We shape experiences to improve lives."[6] The first statement expresses the core value of human centeredness and the goal of using human centeredness to drive technological innovation within the contexts of healthcare and heathy living. The second part focuses on the company ambition to improve the lives of a large number of people.

The Golden Circle framework by Simon Sinek could also be used as a guideline for the content of the different parts of the design direction.[7] The design vision, mission, and principles combined should start by explaining why the design function exists and what its core beliefs are. Then, they should describe how the function should operate and what the core outcomes of its activities will be. The following mission statement by SAP User Experience Design Services offers a good example of how these content elements can be balanced:

> We humanize business software and make innovation real. We apply SAP's Human-Centered Approach to Innovation to transform business data into customer value, based on SAP's Business Technology Platform.[8]

The first part introduces the core belief that technology should be humanized and understood from the perspective of people (the why). The second part refers to SAP's unique and customized approach to innovation (the how). Their webpage features a series of projects to exemplify typical deliverables of the team (the what).

. An important balancing act when working on the content of a design vision, or its mission, is the degree of specificity used to define the scope of design and its ambition over time. For instance, the design mission of a fast-moving consumer goods company focused on the broad and generic goal of contemporizing the nostalgia feeling of the brand and how to bring this to life in new ways. This breadth of scope allows designers to be creative both with how they interpret and use the nostalgia feeling and with the means they use to communicate the brand. In some cases, the design mission or vision needs to be more general than that, to guide the design team to work effectively across the relevant business units. The design director of a consumer packaged goods company pointed out that their design function works well with a fairly generic design mission:

> It's really about improving people's lives. So it has a very generic content. But then every sector makes it a lot more concrete. For example, within the sector of home care, they then identify areas within people's lives where they want to drive innovation.

Finally, the content of the design direction statement is mutable; it must be adjusted periodically to adapt to internal and external change. A review and revision of the design direction should coincide with the strategic agenda of the company. The global design director at a retail company, for example, works in a volatile business context and hence reviews their mission on a yearly basis. One head of design at a software company said that they have a three-year design vision, which remains unchanged during that period and only gets revised when appropriate.

Consistency

The content of the design function's mission and vision should be consistent with the organization's mission and vision, and should illustrate how the design function can contribute to company objectives.

That consistency extends even into the language used to express the design vision, mission, and principles, which should mirror the organization's vocabulary. The CDO of a financial services company clearly described how to use language consistently when translating company values into design values:

> One example: there is the corporate value of "keeping it simple." We actually talked a lot with the executive board about how we just want

to make things clear for people with our services. We consistently refer to the value of design "clarity," which is a specific implementation of simplicity in the context of complicated financial information. Clarity is awesome because we can use it in design critiques. We can say, "How can we make this clearer?" We can use it as a way to prioritize projects, like, "What are the areas that are most confusing?"

The issue of consistency can, however, reveal a duality: on the one hand, leaders need to act as bridges, aligning their approaches (and the design direction) with the organization at large; on the other, they need to work at the forefront of transformation as change agents who find new ways to do things differently. Finding the right balance between aligning with the status quo and being an agent for change is essential. Effective design leaders should build a vision or mission based on what is relevant for the design function while supporting the company strategies, and then socialize it to create alignment in the organization. For example, there was a case of an executive leader who had decided, with the team, to include sustainability in the design vision — long before this was on any corporate agenda. This clear vision to lead sustainability by design steered the company in that direction and later became the springboard for future sustainability efforts by the company. In fact, the design function became the strategic partner to the executive board for sustainability and designed the company playbook on the topic.

Indeed, given designers' ability to envision inspiring future scenarios and synthesize information in a simple yet engaging manner,[9] the process of creating a design vision, mission, and principles can sometimes influence those of the company as well. The VP of business development of a professional services company points out that "design has to help the organization to build the vision. So, the vision of the design function can be, if you want, the vision of the organization." The global head of design at a consumer goods company explained that in their case, a kind of mutual influence flows between the design vision and the company brand. As the company has a strong brand, elements of the brand DNA influenced the design vision and design principles. At the same time, because the company recognizes design as a strategic partner in driving competitive advantage, the direction set by the design vision influences ongoing revisions of the company brand vision and strategy.

Sometimes design is so well-integrated in a business that a separate vision or mission is not needed, especially when design is already an integral part of the business vision. For instance, a design director at a software development and services company explained that the role of design is to add a human dimension to the technology-driven vision of their business:

> What the design team has got involved in is actually giving the human story of why this technology matters to the world, and to people, and overall providing the human framework for that vision. As we are constantly aware of this, and of why we are in this business at a human level, there was no need for a separate vision.

Similarly, the maturity of the company might determine whether there is need for a separate design vision, mission, or principles. The head of design of an e-commerce company explained that, as the company is relatively young and focused on one main product, having a separate design vision would be overkill. Instead, the design function participated in the construction of the overall company vision, which was an intense and very collaborative process, "where design and all other functions connected to the product are working very much together, to map out how we can realize what we want to achieve in the future."

PURSUING THE DIRECTION: CRAFTING A LONG-TERM STRATEGY AND ROADMAP

Once the design vision, mission, and principles have been defined, the executive design leader should begin to plan how to fulfill them. Three additional reference documents are needed: a long-term strategy (three to five years), a design roadmap of how to get there (three to five years), and an annual operational plan that reflects the first step of the roadmap. The three-to-five-year design strategy should focus on the aspirational goals of the design function and be aligned with the strategic plans of the company. The roadmap should provide a temporal perspective on the design strategy, by indicating the steps that should be taken for the coming years to realize the strategy. The annual plan will be more operational, focused on defining design activities and scoping related design investments to allow the design function to engage effectively in the company's annual strategy and operational planning process.

Developing a long-term strategy should be a priority. Working on it allows the executive design leader to take time to reflect and to formalize a plausible and structured course of action for the design function, instead of improvising and using an opaque or ad hoc approach. Furthermore, it is a great starting point for strategic conversations with organizational stakeholders, through which design leaders can demonstrate relevancy, commitment, competence, and business acumen.

Once the strategic priorities of the company and its growth ambitions are set, design leaders should align their design strategy accordingly. The strategy should be directly linked to relevant elements from the company strategy, such as key priorities and goals that might influence the design function (for example, the adoption of a certain culture or transformational program). For instance, the global design director of a consumer-packaged goods company aligned the vision and planning of the design function with the company's aim to increase the repeat purchases of its brands:

> The company vision was to increase repeat purchases. You also need to look at it as a team, from that perspective. Because you are a team, you're in charge of driving growth through design, so you need to know your numbers and you need to know how you are impacting the growth of the overall team.

The head of design at an automotive company explained how the strategy of the design team was kept aligned with the brand values of the company and how design initiatives were defined accordingly. Deriving the design strategy from the brand values is typical for companies operating with longer product cycles:

> You can see how we developed a strategy based on the values of the brand, how we executed it through the concept cars, how we

translated this into our production vehicles, and how the sales results illustrate the effectiveness of the project.

After briefly summarizing relevant company, business, and functional objectives for reference, the design strategy document should cover the long-term objectives of the design function itself. The steps that the design function must take every year to reach their strategic objectives should be described in the roadmap, a tool to explain how to connect the present and the desired state of the design function. For instance, a five-year strategy for achieving design excellence could be translated into a five-year roadmap that includes the following steps:

1. Educate others about design and create awareness for where design can contribute to the success of the company
2. Cultivate the design competencies needed to actively demonstrate the value of design on the job
3. Integrate design approaches into relevant organizational processes, including innovation, market introduction, and strategic planning
4. Establish engagement with design across the organization to become a recognized and trusted partner for core business and company activities
5. Establish global design function leadership, so that decision making, budget ownership, and design thought leadership are formalized, managed, and owned by design

The roadmap breaks down the strategy from a temporal as well as an activity perspective. The yearly steps should be detailed in relation to the various activities the design leader is engaged in. Some examples of activities might be developing processes and tools, developing design competencies, achieving design thought leadership, securing budget ownership, consolidating design governance, appointing design leadership, or establishing strategic design partnerships.

The time horizon for the design strategy and roadmap — preferably three to five years — should, of course, be aligned with the strategy cycle of the organization and reflect the company's ambitions, but it should also anticipate future industry market dynamics. For instance, the CDO of a financial services company indicated that the company uses a three-year strategy cycle. On that basis, and on the design team's intention to anticipate future market and technology dynamics, the design strategy team intentionally fixed three- to ten-year horizons. The three-year horizon was to be used to run the design function in alignment with the rest of the company, while the longer ten-year horizon would be used for research and design concepts tapping into more exploratory future scenarios that could eventually influence and inspire the overall company strategy. In the words of the CDO, "The idea is to give a challenging future statement back to the strategy of the bank and, in this way, help us adjust and de-risk our own design strategy."

In some cases, design leaders might work for companies with a short-term focus (such as fast-moving consumer goods) or even no well-defined long-term strategy. In many cases, this short-term focus is a consequence of companies' need to be reactive to the rapidly changing market and technology dynamics of certain industries and management adopting an agile approach in their strategic planning as a consequence.[10] Design leaders should adapt to that and embrace a similar flexibility, by reviewing and eventually adjusting their strategic documents frequently. However, companies with a short-term orientation might miss out on opportunities in the marketplace if they are simply reactive and operate ad hoc. In order to create increased business sustainability, more proactive planning still needs to be in place to prepare longer-term activities and investments, for example exploring new technology innovations, developing new capabilities, or assessing future partnerships and acquisitions. The design function can explore these themes and build scenarios for discussion and valuation with senior business leaders that could trigger a more strategic approach towards the future planning activities of the company.

EXECUTING THE LONG-TERM STRATEGY: THE ANNUAL OPERATIONAL PLAN

Once a three- to five-year strategy and a roadmap are in place, the executive design leader should engage in translating these documents into an operational plan each year, for the following year. Developing and executing a well-thought-out operational plan that is aligned with the business goals of the company is fundamental for the executive design leader to optimize design resources and enable relevant action. At the same time, putting the plan together will entail dialogue about how to align the design function agenda with the rest of the company, by focusing its annual work on high-priority programs that serve the function and the company. To reach these goals, the operational plan should

- set the priorities and the overall themes for the coming year (such as specific business, innovation, or brand programs; international expansion; efficiency initiatives);
- quantify the enabling investments at the company level and specific business level, and also for geographic locations where design is expected to contribute and deliver support;
- indicate the yearly design objectives and key initiatives, including metrics.

Combining the annual objectives, metrics, and budget for the design function — including, for example, the number of insourced versus outsourced design projects for each business unit, any additional talent, or investment for new space — is always a balancing act requiring design leaders to prioritize and emphasize the value of design. The CDO of a furniture company explained that

there is always a tension — in many ways a healthy tension — as business partners always ask for more programs to reach new customer segments or deliver new solutions to customers. They look for new products, new programs, yet don't necessarily arrive with more money from the business to pay for the [design] resources to execute. The tension is always related to prioritization. Which are the key pieces to execute for the business? Which projects from the past should be let go of in order to tackle important new challenges?

The experience of the general manager of design at a professional service company is similar:

I can decide how I want to scale my team in my annual planning process. For instance, I can decide that there is opportunity to grow by 20 percent. But then, based on that, I will have to hit certain revenue numbers. . . . So if I'm hitting all my numbers around revenues, if I'm hitting all my utilization targets, if everything is in the green, I can go ahead and hire. If, however, this is not the case, that will basically mean I will have to make a business case as to why I want to bring on more people when, for instance, I've got people on the bench who aren't working.

The number of projects per year requested by the businesses has to be balanced with global design team capacity. The level of investment to deliver the full annual design plan created with the business partners takes priority, which means potentially hiring additional designers in-house, outsourcing design activities, or putting projects on hold. When the operational plan calls for a decrease in design programs in the coming year, there will be less call for designers. If this is the case, then a discussion about utilizing that overcapacity is important so that designers are not let go because of a temporary imbalance in the offer and demand for design capacity.

In terms of operational plan content, the list of overarching design objectives might be broken down into three groups:

- *Business design objectives*: These drive the business outcomes and are defined by design leaders and main business stakeholders together. This list of objectives summarizes design team goals across business units or at corporate level — for example, that a certain percentage of design projects will actively gain and utilize insights from customer experiences, or X number of businesses will use Y design tool (for example, co-creation workshops) or cultivate Z design value (for example, collaboration).
- *Design functional objectives*: These drive design function outcomes and are defined by the executive design leader with the design leadership team. Attaining them serves to develop the design function overall (in line with company objectives). Examples are adopting and incorporating new design tools, optimizing an

aspect of the design process, optimizing design capabilities, or expanding team diversity.

- *Personal design objectives*: These objectives are set for individual designers. They should translate functional objectives into professional development goals — design managers might seek to cultivate new leadership skills, designers could enter design award competitions, senior designers can coach junior designers, or design and creative leaders could seek ways to improve their status as thought leaders internally and externally.

Combining objectives from all three categories will yield a set of annual objectives on an individual level for every member of the design team. This way, a healthy balance is guaranteed between business, functional, and personal objectives to strive for, while guaranteeing relevant value creation.

One way to obtain alignment among businesses, wider organizational functions, and regions is by arranging the development of the annual operational plan in a sequential manner — otherwise known as a cascading process. First comes defining annual strategies and priorities at the company level, and then translating these into business and functional objectives. Once the business and functional objectives have been defined, the design leadership team translates them into specific design objectives that, together, make up the annual operational plan. Company strategies are translated into design functional objectives by the executive design leader, and business objectives are translated by the design leaders working for different businesses (or business units) into design objectives relevant to their activities. All of this will be combined and consolidated into a list of annual design objectives. Once design has reached a sufficient level of maturity in the organization, the executive design leader will participate in, influence the discussion about, and help define both corporate and business objectives. If design has not reached maturity, one of the design leader's objectives should be to participate in and contribute to those processes. If design leaders are excluded from the process of defining business (unit) objectives,

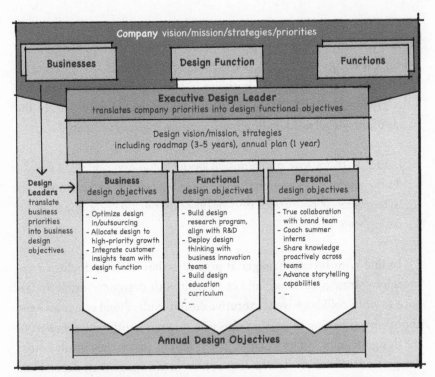

FIGURE 3.2. Cascading company priorities to business, functional, and design objectives as part of the annual business planning cycle.

the objectives and needs of the design function may not be perceived as relevant and may not receive the attention from business managers that is their due.

Defining design objectives at the individual designer level is the last step of the cascading sequence; once the business objectives and the design functional objectives have been defined, they directly inform designers' personal objectives. This translation is particularly important, as it makes the design operations plan and its yearly execution tangible and engaging for the design team — especially those not involved in the making of the strategy. Establishing these objectives is also important for design performance management (there will be more on this topic in Chapter 6, "Design Resources"). Figure 3.2 summarizes the cascading process of the annual business planning cycle.

CREATING DIRECTION: ENGAGEMENT APPROACHES

Several executive design leaders indicated in their interviews that establishing the design direction is one of their core responsibilities. Executive design leaders should take the initiative in starting the process of creating a design direction and choose the most suitable approach to that. In the words of the global head of design of a consumer goods company,

> I see it . . . as my task, as the design leader in this company. . . . I feel it's my role and my responsibility to lead the way, to already come with new ideas, new visions and initiatives before the company starts asking for it.

In line with recent managerial practices that favor an inclusive approach to strategy making,[11] and consistent with designers' usual preference to work collaboratively, executive design leaders tend to use an open approach to creating the design direction, engaging different members of the design team in different ways. The extent to which they involve other design leaders in their strategizing process and engagement depends on two factors: the degree of design function maturity and strategic experience within the organization, and the various elements of the design direction.

To assess the maturity and experience of the design function, and that of design leaders and design team members, the following criteria should be considered:

- To what extent does the team share a common understanding of the future of design, the core strategic activities, and how to collaborate with and add value to other functions?
- How experienced are the design leaders in functional planning?
- Which well-established design processes exist in and across functions and businesses? To what extent have they been deployed?
- Where does the design function sit on the spectrum between the operational (short term, ad hoc) and the strategic (design applied across every function, business or activity, region)?
- How many trusted, long-standing partnerships does the design function have with other company functions? Does it work with

marketing to define and implement branding strategies? Does it work with HR to build and implement design taxonomies and diversity strategies? Does it work with R&D to explore and frame innovation strategies?

- Has the design functional governance model (design sponsoring, reporting lines, and physical location) been implemented? (See Chapter 4, "Design Organization," for more on this).

The second factor implies making a distinction between the strategic components of the design direction (the vision, or mission, and long-term strategy of design) and the operational ones (annual operational plan, roadmap, design principles). Using different strategizing approaches depending on the nature of the design direction components reflects recent trends in corporate strategy making. Specifically, some companies split the strategizing process into two distinct streams: one focused on current business, one focused on future moves that may call for different team configurations and different approaches.[12]

Table 3.1 summarizes the different engagement approaches that result from the combination of these two factors.

When an experienced team of design leaders is in place, a co-creative approach to the strategic components of the design direction can be very effective. Seasoned leaders understand the organizational context and have the experience to co-create the design direction at the appropriate level of strategic abstraction. Co-creation is particularly beneficial when the executive design leader wants to obtain widespread buy-in within the design leadership team and the company at large. For this reason the VP of design for a healthcare company developed a design vision together with

TABLE 3.1. Engagement approaches when developing the design direction.

	Low Maturity or Experience	High Maturity or Experience
Strategic direction	Create engage through implementation	Co-create with design leaders
Operational plan	Iterate with design team	Collaborate with design team

the design leadership team. This required a longer development time due to the need of gathering and harmonizing all the inputs, but led to a powerful and resilient outcome which is still shared and used after five years.

When design maturity has sufficiently advanced within the organization, the co-creative approach to composing strategic documents can extend beyond the design function. For instance, the CDO of a PC hardware peripherals company explained that there is much conversation going on between the CDO and the CEO — the line of communication is direct. The design strategy logically flows from this continuous dialogue; it truly is co-created. "It's more of an ongoing dialogue than, sort of, me going away and doing my own thing then coming back and saying, 'Ta-da, here you go, what do you think?'"

In some cases, when executive design leaders have just started their assignments, they may still have to build their leadership team with the necessary level of maturity and experience to support the formulation of the strategic components of the design direction. More specifically, the design leadership team might still need to develop the appropriate strategic acumen. Involving them in the design direction's strategic co-creative process might lead to ineffective dialogue on design strategies. Furthermore, there may be a lot of team engagement, but in this case that comes with the risk of a compromised outcome. In this context, a less inclusive, "closed" approach might be more appropriate. Design leaders may wish to independently create the strategic components of the design direction, involve the design leadership team to refine them, and involve the entire design team to implement them. One of the interviewed executive design leaders found exactly this context when starting a leadership assignment, and opted to draft the three-to-five-year design strategy independently, on the basis of previous experience. Afterward, the first version of the strategy was presented, to get feedback from the design team and adjust the strategy accordingly. Here are some of the questions to ask the design team to obtain useful feedback:

- How will the design strategy impact the company at large?
- How will the design strategy impact the business (unit) you work for? What challenges and opportunities do you foresee in your business context?

- How will the design strategy impact your personal work as a designer? Does the strategy support a creative, supportive environment? Can your practice expand through it?
- How can we enrich this design strategy?
- What are your main concerns regarding this design strategy?
- How can you personally contribute to the success of the design strategy?

The more operational elements of the design direction will call for input from the entire design team (instead of only the leadership team), because these will have a direct impact on design operations and the designers are experts in this area. When the design team has an appropriate level of experience and maturity, the design leader can define annual design objectives in collaboration with the entire team, and everyone can agree on how to reach those objectives realistically. As the general manager of design of a professional services company explained,

We presented our design objectives to the whole team, and then we broke them down into "hot topic" categories. And then we had the team go away and work on statements in terms of how we might deliver on some of those key topics. That then became a set of initiatives and activities that we would do to help us get there.

When the design team is still growing and gaining experience, then an iterative approach to developing operational elements is appropriate. Executive design leaders and their leadership teams take the lead in developing a first version of these documents, quickly share them with the rest of the design team, and iterate on them during their implementation, on the basis of the feedback and the learnings of the design team while using them.

Executive design leaders need to adjust their engagement approach over time. For example, in an organization in which design is relatively immature, an executive design leader can start with a more autonomous way of defining the design direction and, over time, shift the approach to a more collaborative one once design has matured in terms of strategic capability. As noted by a VP of design from an automotive company, doing this requires the "mental flexibility" to constantly adjust and redefine professional activities according to changing circumstances.

COMMUNICATING THE DESIGN DIRECTION

Once the components of the design direction have been crafted, the executive design leader needs to think about how to communicate and share them effectively within and outside the design function.

This should be an ongoing process for two reasons. First, large organizations are characterized by a frequent turnover of in-house design staff, and, to a greater extent, by ongoing turnover in management. The global design director of a retailing company explained, "I communicate the mission frequently because there is a turnover in this company. So I have to present it to someone almost every week." Second, because the goal of a clear and inspiring design direction is also to create buy-in within the organization, the same message might need to be repeated again and again, consistently, to generate resonance and normalize or socialize its momentum. A head of design operating in the aerospace industry explained,

> What we do is periodically go round the different functions, or where we see a need, and we give a presentation to say, "This is the creative design function, this is why we do what we do, this is how we do it and where, and this is what it means to you." We use the strategy, the mission, and a vision as tools to explain to our colleagues who we are, what we do, and how we can help.

To communicate the message consistently, design leaders should be simple, clear, and concise. The head of design from the aerospace industry uses an adaptable slide deck of just six slides, for example. Other design leaders use brochures, leaflets, sketches of visualizations, and videos.

The design leader should adapt the content and format of the message to each specific audience. If the audience is senior (business) managers, sharing the core beliefs and the scope of the design function is most appropriate, so they are inspired to explore and can grasp the implications of a collaboration with design. When the audience is the design team, communication should focus on the "how" of the vision, mission, and values, to guide prospective behaviors and activities. If the audience includes other functions or business units, emphasizing the "what" of design — outcomes — is more relevant, to manage and hence concretize expectations.

Design leaders should make optimal use of their visualization and storytelling skills as they create these platforms. Several design leaders indicated that when the goal is to communicate the direction to the designers in the team, expressing the design vision, mission, and/or principles in the form of a manifesto might be more effective to inspire and create engagement. A manifesto uses a compelling, figurative, inspirational tone of voice to communicate intentions and aims — it is a statement of intent, and a means of exploring responses to that statement. An effective design manifesto must therefore use powerful and visual language to convey its message. For instance, in 2015, to celebrate its ninetieth anniversary, Philips Design chose a video as a visually and verbally engaging means of communicating their design manifesto.[13] Through a combination of animation and storytelling, the video reaches the goal of engaging both the team and an external audience about what design at Philips entails and what core principles drive the design function. When the goal is to communicate the design direction to an internal business audience, a simpler format and more relevant language are best.

A well-thought-out and well-executed format ensures effective and memorable communication. However, the design director at the aforementioned consumer goods company also highlighted some drawbacks to overly curating content, noting that a more open-ended document and the feeling of it being a rough draft gave designers the feeling they could "actually jump into it, roll around, influence, and be part of it." The CDO of a furniture company made hand-drawn illustrations to explain the ambitions of the design function to top management in a tangible, inviting manner.

Certain elements of the design direction should also be communicated to the outside world to give visibility and a clear positioning to the design function and establish thought leadership. Many design leaders indicated that having a part of the company website dedicated to the design function is a valuable and effective means of communicating the design direction and position of the role of design within the organization and to the outside world. The timing used to roll out these kinds of external communication requires careful consideration — normalizing the design direction internally is more important. More specifically, before sharing the inspirational components of design direction externally, a design leader should ensure that the design direction is known and embraced by the design team and the rest of the organization, and well aligned with the mission and strategy of the company as a whole.

MONITORING THE PROGRESS OF THE DESIGN FUNCTION

Once the design direction has been defined and translated into a roadmap and operational plan, the executive design leader will monitor the yearly progress of its implementation and demonstrate its impact year after year. To this end, the design leadership team should agree on a set of metrics to use and include them in the annual operational plan. In recent years there have been several studies attempting to identify metrics that could be generally and reliably used to monitor design function performance.[14] The best metrics to use, and whether to use them to monitor the design function, are hot topics among design leaders. Monitoring the value of design through clear, quantifiable, business-driven metrics is an important task of the design leader, according to many of them, to gain and maintain organizational stakeholders' commitment to investing in design. For instance, the VP of design of a healthcare company said that in their organization, the design direction focuses on results:

> What have we landed? How many projects? How much value have we created? Every year I create a yearbook for the business that shows yearly progress. . . . It's really important that we don't fall in love with design, and "design-ness," and that we show how it can solve business problems, and deliver financial revenue for its investment.

According to the CDO of a financial services company, being able to provide a business case for design might be important when design has not yet reached maturity in the organization, to grow its budget:

> I would say that almost the entire first year was building the business case. When I was hired, the company had no plan for the headcount I would need, the budget I would receive, or how design as a function should be shaped. That was both a gift — because I could shape

everything myself — and a curse, because I had to build all the momentum myself, through a lot of work on the business case.

Since the value and success of design are highly dependent on its level of integration, organizational innovation capacity, and branding activities, it is very difficult to measure the sole contribution design makes to business success. Instead of trying to measure the (economic) business value of design, it is often more effective to measure the progress of the design function qualitatively. How mature is it (for example in terms of resources and scale)? Where on the roadmap do its activities sit? How well has design been integrated into business operations? R&D? marketing?

Qualitative assessment is an effective way to demonstrate and measure the progress of the design function on the basis of tangible design activities initiated and owned by the design function. The different perspectives and best practices that the design leaders interviewed use to monitor and measure the progress of the design function are listed here, as a set of guidelines.

- *The ensemble of metrics used should combine the quantitative and qualitative.* For instance, the global design director of a retailing company combined qualitative metrics such as "(improved) customer perceptions," "(scope of) design culture," and "extent of brand equity stewardship" with traditional quantitative metrics such as sales and cost reductions. A VP of design at an automotive parts company assesses design function performance by combining sales data with subjective assessments of market reactions to design work. For instance, "customer testimonials, verbatim" and "media responses to press conferences and press releases" are used to complement traditional quantitative data.
- *Business metrics should be translated into design metrics.* Design has only a partial influence — which it cannot entirely own — on business metrics. Design-specific metrics, linked to the metrics of the company or business unit, are more useful. For instance, the senior design director of a consumer electronics company started from the strategic goals and metrics of the company — customer

base, repeat purchase, customer satisfaction, and so on — to identify some qualitative design metrics that would reflect the work the
design team had performed and inspire their continued efforts.
"Did design inspire our customers to buy a premium brand? How
easy are our products to use? How much flexibility do they afford to
users?" And because the financial industry focuses heavily on the
Net Promoter Score (NPS),[15] one financial services CDO was developing a similar score for its design function focused on customer
experience and on a set of usability and desirability criteria that
determine the customer experience quality.

- *The ensemble of metrics should assess design integration at three
  levels: project, process, and strategy.* For example, the SVP of design at a telecommunications company was using the NPS in
  combination with assessments measuring design quality against
  specific criteria, customer experience (and confidence in it) at the
  product level, design thinking trainings completed, design methods used by functions other than design, the number of product
  development processes that refer to design at the process level,
  and design's degree of influence on the company roadmap and
  on product portfolio decisions at the strategy level.

CONCLUSION

Setting a course for design and implementing it are central tasks in establishing the foundations for reaching design excellence. A reliable direction
for design as a function must harmonize the function's vision and mission,
principles, long-term strategy, roadmap, and annual operational plan with
overarching company policies and aims. The design executive leader must
continually monitor, obtain feedback on, and update these elements to fuel
the overarching pursuit of design excellence. This final section mentions a
few of the dualities that arise as the executive leader goes about accomplish-
ing this crucial task.

Challenge Versus Adhere

When hired for the job, often executive design leaders are asked to play a
role in facilitating an ambition the company intends to embrace. In order

to succeed at this, executive design leaders and their teams are expected to be change agents. This might result in a vision and strategies that challenge the status quo, which may lead to resistance within the company that stymies progress. To avoid getting bogged down, executive design leaders need to adhere to certain elements of the organization's strategic direction, and at the same time mitigate the risk of diluting the transformative potential of their activities.

Open Versus Closed Strategizing

When working on the different components of the design direction, the executive design leader should assess whether to adopt an open, co-creative approach that includes design team members, or a closed one that involves the design team at a later stage to get feedback and assist with implementation. Even if co-creation comes more naturally to design leaders and triggers ownership of the design direction more immediately, in some circumstances involving the team and engaging in peer collaboration creates a lengthier process and can lead to more mediocre outcomes.

Long-Term Versus Short-Term Perspectives

When developing the direction for the design function, the executive design leader is by definition required to adopt a long-term perspective and develop a thorough plan that covers an extended time horizon (three to five years). A structured, long-term approach is important for two reasons: it enables executive design leaders to express their future ambitions for the design function and explain how those ambitions can be achieved in practice, and it demonstrates leadership to other executives and managers in the company. At the same time, design leaders should take into account that the organization is contending with short-term realities, which requires leaders to constantly recalibrate plans over the long term. A short-term focus may be necessary to competitively respond to a competitive landscape, and to foster the more agile approach to strategizing required to support constantly changing environmental dynamics.

To cope with these three key dualities, design leaders might consider the following guidelines:

- Internalization and normalization should be part of the plan. Executive design leaders should put substantial strategic thought into how, when, and with whom to create and share the strategic direction of design as a function. Sharing the process of developing its strategic direction — including draft versions of it — is an effective way of achieving transparency about the function's ambitions, co-creating them, and garnering engagement and support for them.
- The design strategy should be adaptable. Executive design leaders should be pragmatic and have a mindset that allows for continuous evaluation and adjustment of the design strategy and the related roadmap. Ambitions might need to change as a consequence of the internal challenges of implementing a transformational plan and the volatility of environmental dynamics. The design strategy, roadmap, and annual operational plan ought to be reviewed regularly (once or twice per year), in line with the organization's business planning cycle. The plan must be readily adaptable — while still aiming at a desired end state (the what), there should be realism about the journey itself (the how).
- Long-term ambitions should act as drivers. Deviations from the design direction are to be expected and embraced, when appropriate. However, design leaders and their leadership teams also need to display resilience and demonstrate fearless leadership so they may stay on course and navigate (what often amounts to) short-term distractions from the overarching goal of reaching design function excellence.

Defining and implementing the overall design direction is the core responsibility of the executive design leader. It requires a visionary position about design's future as a function of the organization, an engaging way of communicating this, and the ability to make it actionable. Furthermore, the design direction must be shared with the main stakeholders in the company to ensure alignment, buy-in, and ongoing support. Most important, it has to be internalized by the design team for them to be able to contribute with commitment and motivation to its implementation.

CHAPTER 4

Design Organization

The way design is governed in the organization determines how it is embedded and will give all designers across the company a recognized placeholder to where they belong.

A SOLID FOUNDATION for effective design leadership at scale requires an organizational framework that describes and formalizes how design is managed and will operate. A well-defined organizational framework for design explicates the way the design function will work together with other parts of the organization and its key stakeholders and deals with lines of authority, decision making, and accountability.

Several of the design leaders interviewed said that when they began working at their current jobs, the existing organizational framework for design was inconsistent or had never been formally drafted and implemented. For example, the CDO at a home appliance company encountered a situation in which the functional reporting lines for the design leadership team diverged considerably — some reported directly to the executive managers of their business units, while others reported to managers placed one or two levels down in the organization.[1] This lack of consistency in reporting lines caused confusion and hindered the adoption of a unified view on the value of design within the organization at large.

To help design leaders define a robust organizational framework, this chapter provides guidelines for a structured approach consisting of five activities: scoping, evaluating, exploring, contextualizing, and future-proofing. An organizational framework for design based on this structured approach will answer these key questions:

- Who sponsors design within the organization, and how will design budgets be prioritized and allocated?
- Who manages the designers and their day-to-day design activities? Who reports to whom, and when?
- Where will the design team(s) be physically located?

We first discuss the activities to define a solid organizational framework in more detail. Then we give an overview of the benefits and detriments of different design-sponsoring approaches; consider various ways of configuring lines of authority; describe potential workspace constellations, including their pros and cons; and provide an overview of tactics to implement the organizational framework for design effectively. We conclude with a discussion of the core dualities inherent in design organization and ways to manage these in large, complex companies.

A STRUCTURED APPROACH

One design leader from a consumer goods company stated plainly that their organization completely lacked an overarching, systemic approach to design organization:

> The design community is organized in quite an informal, casual way — also because the scale of design at our company simply doesn't call for a highly structured approach.

However, even if the in-house design team is small, or an ad hoc approach is working for design right now, it is still in the executive design leader's interest to consciously build and implement an appropriate organizational framework to further grow the role of design within the organization.

Using a structured process to develop the framework is strongly recommended — even if what it yields is only used to bolster the rationale to relevant organizational stakeholders that an effective framework is needed. The following activities will guide that process:

- *Scoping*: What is the purpose and scope of design within the organization?
- *Evaluating*: What kind of design organization is currently in place; what are its advantages and disadvantages?
- *Exploring*: Which (elements from) existing frameworks are desirable and can we learn from?
- *Contextualizing*: Which company strategies, priorities, modes of operation, objectives, and constraints are likely to impact the framework for design?
- *Futureproofing*: How can the framework accommodate future organizational objectives and goals?

Figure 4.1 visualizes the logical sequence of these activities. In the next sections, we delve more deeply into each one.

Scoping

An important activity when drawing up a coherent organizational framework is determining the scope of design: what activities will the design function perform in the organization? Chapter 1, "Design Context," gives some examples of what the scope of design can be, while in Chapter 5, "Design Taxonomy," the process of defining the scope of design is described in more detail.

Once the scope has been determined, the executive design leader should identify how the people who fall within that scope fit into the organizational hierarchy and where they are physically located. While this may seem easy, for some executive design leaders working in sizeable and complex organizations it can be quite challenging to identify where the designers are and ought to be — especially when their roles and responsibilities are spread out across different departments and business units. As one VP of design from a computer hardware and software company pointed out,

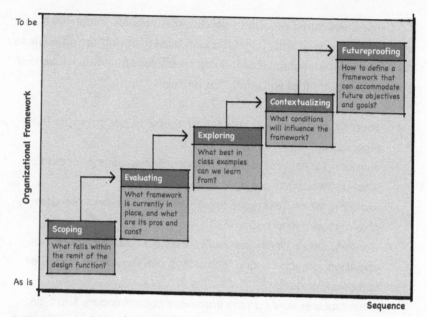

FIGURE 4.1. Activities for defining an effective organizational framework for design.

After being in this role for some time now, I still discover designers working in remote parts of the organization who are not yet formally part of the design function.

Having "unidentified" designers dispersed across the organization is problematic, if only because, as noted by a design leader from a professional services organization, "Design is not talking with design." This person went on to explain that this lack of alignment makes it hard to establish a unified voice for design throughout the organization, which, in turn, hampers effective scaling and value creation.

Evaluating

After defining the scope of the design function inside the organization, the executive design leader can now perform a thorough evaluation of the current organizational framework for design. To collect insights on current practices, they may not just involve individuals formally associated with design — they might include a wide variety of contributors from across the organization, including representatives from the human resources and finance functions, and other relevant department or business unit leaders. These conversations can serve to encourage a range of stakeholders to acknowledge the need to (re)define design governance policy, which in turn can increase confidence and support for the new or revised framework. Internal knowledge databases can also be used as sources of information. For example, enterprise resource planning systems can help identify spending and the amount of resources related to design, but only if those systems have been implemented successfully across every entity in the enterprise globally. Some have argued that when there is no systemwide placeholder for design in the organization's resource system, design investment could be the largest category of spending going unnoticed by the CEO.

Evaluating the status quo will help executive design leaders identify what is broken and what already works well. They will gain valuable insight into what ought to change *and* what they might want to keep as it is. This implies an important edict for the executive design leader: "no change for change's sake." It is better to work within the current structure as much as possible, as it will help win support for an updated or new organizational framework. But when making decisions about what to consolidate and what to change, executive design leaders should also keep the bigger picture in mind, because what is really going well at the moment may not necessarily still work when design is operating at scale.

Exploring

To gather diverse ideas for the desired future state of the design organization, executive design leaders can cast a net far wider than their own leadership teams and involve different leaders from across the organization. They may also draw inspiration from the organizational frameworks used by other leading companies that have already formalized design within their operations. This chapter provides some guidance by summarizing the frameworks we encountered in our research.

Contextualizing

While a design organization adopted elsewhere may provide inspiration, using preexisting frameworks from other organizations in a carbon copy way is not advisable — the organizational context should be the guide to establish the core characteristics of the framework and to ensure that the framework can work effectively within the organization. As noted by the president of the Design Management Institute and her colleague: "[T]here is no standard off-the-shelf template for the perfect design organization; success depends on aligning the role of the design function with the organization's strategic objectives and then tailoring everything else to suit."[2]

For example, Spotify's organizational structure revolves around small multifunctional teams (squads) that have the authority to make their own decisions. Recognizing the need to establish design consistency, the online streaming service established a Design Ops team, responsible for developing companywide best-in-class design tools and systems. But this top-down approach did not work within Spotify's culture of self-determination. As the head of Spotify's Design Ops team said, "Spotify values a good deal of autonomy and encourages teams to solve problems in their own way — so we needed to tread lightly at first."[3] Other Spotify design leaders involved in a project intended to establish greater consistency in its internal design language also stressed the importance of understanding "the company's characteristics and peculiarities" and adapting to them on the basis of earlier, failed attempts to establish unity. As a result, rather than being a single entity, the current design language system is configured as a family of systems. Furthermore, the general approach of the Design Ops team is bottom-up — they co-create alongside designers sourced from the broader organization and have adopted an influence approach rather than an enforcement approach to foster design consistency.[4]

Within large companies, the organizational framework for design often operates within a broader matrix-based structure. A matrix is a grid-like organizational structure that allows a company to address various business dimensions using multiple leadership structures. A matrix can take a variety of forms, but the basic structure is typically organized across two dimensions: business (products) and regions, or business (products) and departments or functions. A matrix allows the organization to focus on multiple business goals and can also facilitate information flow, enable economies of scale, and enhance innovation and response time. Utilizing a matrix may also reveal challenges, such as potentially conflicting goals, unclear roles and responsibilities, ambiguous lines of authority, and silo-focused activities.[5] Recently, organizations have been experimenting with new ways to organize the matrix in an effort to address some of its weaknesses.[6] Drafting a clearly defined organizational framework for design, or clarifying an earlier version, may actually give executive management the impetus it needs to redefine the overarching organizational structure.

Futureproofing

Defining an organizational framework for design means "futureproofing" it — will it retain its pertinence over the medium term (three to five years) in the face of anticipated contextual fluctuations, stressors, and advances? Executive design leaders should structure the new (or redesigned) framework so that it anticipates possible future expansion in design within the organization and can adapt sustainably to changes to the organization's overall structure and operations. Such vision is akin to the notion of "thinking big." To rephrase acclaimed personal development expert David Schwartz, a big thinker visualizes what can be done in the future and is not stuck in the present.[7] Design leaders should, however, always align their framework with overarching company strategies — proposing an organizational framework that does not align with these strategies will not receive appreciation and support from key stakeholders and will therefore not be endorsed. More on tactics to facilitate alignment and implementation can be found later in this chapter.

SPONSORSHIP OF DESIGN

To define a cohesive organizational framework, a key question to answer is how design will be sponsored, and by whom. Design sponsorship refers to the ways the design function is funded and supported within the organization. Different sponsorship approaches are possible; they can be clustered into these three basic approaches:[8]

- *Approach 1: Business unit sponsorship*: design decentralized into the organization's line of businesses
- *Approach 2: Corporate sponsorship*: design as a central, corporate function

- *Approach 3: Hybrid sponsorship*: combination business unit and corporate sponsorship

Approach 1: Business Unit Sponsorship

In this approach, design funding is included in the business unit's financial plans — investments connected with design are an integral part of the business unit's annual budget. Whether design is integrated into one, several, or all of the organization's business unit budgets depends on the extent of its scale and whether or not every business unit will need design support.

When design is fully integrated within a business unit, the investments tend to be historical and incremental — in other words, the annual budget that will cover all the investments for design is rolled forward from the prior year. Decisions to add or subtract from design's annual operating budget are made by business unit leadership, typically during annual budget planning. A design leader is preferably part of the business unit leadership team to support prioritization of design investment. Overall, budget discussions tend to involve trade-off conversations during which decisions are made about projects or activities that need design support (and to what extent) to optimize the business unit's outcomes. When making trade-off decisions, the leadership team must prioritize projects and activities that contribute to fulfilling the strategic plans of the business unit and the overarching corporate strategies set out by the CEO.

One furniture company CDO pointed out that when design is sponsored by a business unit, leaders are more likely to make measured decisions about design, because satisfying their appetite for design has clear and direct financial consequences. On the other hand, when design is covered by the corporate budget, business units may utilize more design resources than they truly require, because they do not have to pay directly for them. Put differently, design being covered by business unit budgets can lead to more effective and efficient utilization of the organization's designers.

Another benefit offered by direct business unit sponsorship of design is that it can result in greater overall commitment to design and more engagement by senior leadership. Rather than representing a fragmented use of resources, design can occupy a more prominent place within the structure of the organization. And rather than design tasks being simply operational, they can evolve to become more strategic. Design reveals itself more as a core strategic competency, rather than an off-the-shelf competency that can easily be in- and outsourced. When design is made an integral part of business unit budgets, it becomes a long-term investment, similar to R&D. That investment is less likely to be discontinued on the basis of short-term financial challenges. As Eric observed during one of the interviews,

> Design, similar to R&D, is a long-term investment. It ought not to be switched on and off as a response to short-term realities. In order to leverage these investments into effective and impactful ones over time, a long-term mindset is definitely called for.

Core leadership begins to realize that design drives value, not cost, when this approach to sponsorship has been adopted.

Some responsibilities do appear when design is completely integrated into business unit budgets. One is the enduring accountability of demonstrating to leadership that investments in design directly impact business results. Ultimately, leadership has a finite amount of financial means and has to prioritize investment in a way that will maximize outcomes. For example, one design director who was part of a business leadership team noted that every year, during budget discussions, there was a need to demonstrate that design was "moving the needle." And the VP of design at a technology company shared that demonstrating the value of design is especially critical when business leaders are not accustomed to investing in design:

> We need to continually make the case . . . that design is driving business results. And if it's not, or if we can't make that case — especially as the new kids on the block — then they're going to assign their funding somewhere else.

Approach 2: Corporate Sponsorship
In this approach, design funding is centralized, similar to other areas typically organized in this way — HR, finance, legal, facilities management.

When design is prioritized as a corporate function, two basic frameworks emerge.

Funding Approach 2a: Centralized Design

Design investment in this approach is entirely covered by the company's budget. That budget, in turn, is paid for with corporate "taxes" on the various business units in the organization. The company's design budget is usually determined annually and monitored monthly. Design budgets may increase or decrease over time, as budget prioritization takes place at the more centralized level and will depend on (estimated) company results. During budget allocation discussions, the executive design leader will prepare a design plan to validate the proposed design budget, similar to other department heads whose budgets are sponsored centrally. Solid arguments are those tightly linked to the strategic goals of the organization. The design leader will have to translate strategic goals into budgetary implications: which design resources will be needed to make these goals a reality?

With this centralized funding approach, the executive design leader is the owner of the design resources and manages their utilization according to an annual plan agreed upon with main leadership stakeholders. Departments or business units receive allocations for design resources based on priorities all parties have agreed to. One design director shared that the centralized funding approach at their organization had created a "somewhat competitive atmosphere" among project teams:

> The teams have to demonstrate a real necessity for design, first of all, and then prove that if they are given design resources, their case for leveraging those resources to create more value is solid.

Overall, when prioritizing design resource allocation, a design leader needs to think strategically, and not only take into account short-term organizational or design goals. This type of strategic thinking is exemplified by one head of design from a financial services organization:

> I always think about how we can strategically use our designers; I want to put them on areas that are either very strategic for us, or

where we want to move parts of the business forward. I always align [my decisions] with the strategic priorities of the business and how we can get the most value out of the designers on our team.

When an executive design leader centrally manages design budget allocation, they have more agility and flexibility in terms of utilizing design resources. Once a project is completed and/or there is a pressing need for design resources elsewhere, a design leader can release designers from one project to work on another. This is also possible because business leaders are less likely "to cling" to specific designers as their capacity is managed and prioritized by the design function.

There are some challenges to this approach. First and foremost is that design might be perceived as an overhead cost rather than as an investment related to value creation. That cost perception may then have ramifications on the organization's longer-term commitment to design. If support for design at the corporate level is discontinued, the business units might not step up funding accordingly, especially if they have not sufficiently experienced how well design drives results. One design leader pointed out that when design is financed centrally, the head of design must constantly ensure that the voice of the business is represented, and that designers are not perceived as "designing for the sake of design." What this means is that design can appear "remote" and disconnected from business priorities and strategies.

Overall, this centralized funding approach is particularly appropriate when design is still emerging as a function or area of activity within the organization — when it has no track record yet in demonstrating its ability to create value. Once that record stands, and there is an established design culture and a critical mass of support, it may be appropriate to decentralize design and have it incorporated into individual business budgets.

Funding Approach 2b: Design as Internal Design Consultancy

This approach is known as the consultancy or "pay-to-play" approach. Designers are allocated to work using time increment agreements based on project requirements. In order to invoice project costs, designers are expected to keep track of their project activities by "time writing," as is common in the consulting industry. At the start of each budget cycle, the design leadership team plans out the anticipated design service volume for the different areas of organization according to its capacity. This funding approach means that the design function does not represent a corporate cost center, as it does in the centralized design approach. It acts as its own cost center, normally using a zero-profit agreement if services are only intended to meet internal design demands. As a result, the design leader needs to put substantial effort into closely managing offer and demand — this is especially true given organizations' constant dynamic realities and evolving plans.

Sometimes the design function is also encouraged to work for third-party clients. Working for these third party-clients can bring a range of opportunities, including

- attracting top talent because of the potential to work for multiple brands and markets on diverse projects;
- gaining new insights into adjacent technologies, industries, and markets;
- gathering additional revenue that can be reinvested into the design function;
- positioning design internally through building a portfolio of case studies reflecting the work done for premium clients;
- professionalizing the design function in a competitive market environment where clients have a choice to work with any consultancy.

Working for external clients may, however, also divert focus and resources from internal organizational priorities or even create potential conflicts of interest that can be a challenge to manage effectively. A good rule of thumb is to avoid working for clients on products or services that directly compete with those from your own organization.

One of the biggest disadvantages of the "pay-to-play" approach is that it comes with a lot of internal administrative, transactional, and compliance challenges, which results in scarce design resources being dedicated to noncreative activities. For example, substantial time will be needed to scope projects with internal and external clients and track design hours per project in order to invoice projects correctly. One design director working at a professional services organization that recently changed its organizational framework for design, adopting a "pay-to-play" model, had this to say: "A lot of time gets wasted now with justifying design hours." The director also noted that working this way can be demoralizing. "It kills our souls a little bit, because, for us, our job is not simply about results — about profit and loss — it is about the purpose and feeling proud of what we do."

Another consequence of the "pay-to-play" funding approach is that it can make designers feel as though what they do is not valued by the organization — they are merely project-based service providers, rather than strategic assets. Designers exert a less substantial impact on strategic direction; they are contracted into business projects after decisions have been made about which product or market opportunities to pursue. The role of design becomes therefore predominantly tactical, in this case. The consultancy model — with its constant temperature taking and micromanagement — may give the impression that the organization marginally trusts design to deliver efficient and effective results. This, in turn, can limit design leaders' capacity to attract and retain talent.

Approach 3: Hybrid Sponsorship

The most common sponsorship approach in our research was a hybrid one, which might be described as "centrally decentralized." In this approach, the majority of design is paid for out of individual business unit budgets, but there is also a small, centralized design team whose activity is covered by the organization's overall operating budget. This small, centralized design team acts as a center for excellence and may be responsible for activities that relate to the following:

- *Vision and strategy*: drafting long-term strategic goals and ambitions for the design function and the roadmap to reach them
- *Communication and positioning*: thought leadership on design and design positioning, including sharing of best cases related to design-related themes to inspire both internal and external stakeholders
- *Exploration and research*: future design program initiation and coordination, knowledge creation of newly emerging design

competency areas, insight into themes relevant at the greater organizational level or across organizational departments and teams globally

- *Operations and compliance*: design efficiency capture and replication at scale and design management according to the organization's compliance standards
- *Learning and development*: talent development, clear design career path creation, ongoing design competency development, and succession planning
- *Culture and community*: design community creation and activation within the organization, social activity and design-related event organization for designers spread across the organization, cultivation of a strong creative culture and a sense of purpose and belonging
- *Tools and systems*: establishment of best-practice design processes, methods, and tools that create and maintain design consistency and replicability, facilitate design management at the global organizational level, and are resilient enough to accommodate ongoing changes.

The center of design excellence is normally headed by the executive design leader in their capacity of the organization's head of design. However, a centrally funded design center may be more operational, less strategic in nature, and hence not guided by the executive design leader, like the Design Ops team at Spotify.[9] In a different hybrid funding variation, corporate funding for design is more substantial; it covers not only the costs related to the center of excellence but also the costs for a certain percentage of designers who can flexibly perform activities for individual business units. A design leader whose DIY company employs this variation described it like this:

The designers paid out of the corporate budget are a pool of talent that I manage for the business units. . . . I negotiate with our business units what's required, in terms of design input, to reach the goals set for them by the CEO.

Any hybrid approach means that the design leader has a flexible team of designers who are deployed according to demand. That flexibility allows for better design talent management, because designers can be allocated to projects and activities across several units.

Table 4.1 presents an overview of the key characteristics of decentralized, centralized, and hybrid sponsorship approaches.

REPORTING LINES
Reporting Lines Within the Design Function

Large, complex organizations often use a matrix reporting structure — employees can report to multiple managers, either via solid (direct, primary) reporting lines, or dotted (indirect, secondary) lines. This solid and dotted reporting structure is also referred to as dual reporting.

A solid-line manager, from an administrative and oversight perspective, is the primary manager. They set tasks, supervise, and review the performance of their direct reports. Dotted-line managers have a secondary relationship with their indirect reports. They might assign specific project deliverables to indirect reports, and subsequently review and provide feedback on the (interim) outcomes. Dotted-line managers tend to drive priorities and objectives by exerting an informal influence in collaboration with a solid-line manager.[10]

An executive design leader must clearly establish the reporting lines for the designers when defining design governance. Who is accountable for what? To whom? To answer this, design leaders who work within a matrix structure must ascertain whether a dual reporting structure — combining a dotted-line and a solid-line manager — is effective. Having a single, solid reporting line is best, because the person driving priorities, setting goals, doing performance reviews, and managing opportunities for professional development is transparent to the designers. In some cases, however, there can be good reasons for additional reporting lines to be put in place.

When making decisions regarding reporting lines and accountability, the most basic criterion guiding the decision should be, Who is the sponsor? Sponsorship often entails direct reporting so that designers' efforts serve the sponsor's priorities and objectives. But even if design is a component of business unit budgets, it is important to establish and maintain

TABLE 4.1. Three design sponsorship approaches, including their key characteristics.

Sponsorship Type	Business	Corporate		Hybrid
Funding approach	**Approach 1:** Distributed funding Design funded through business unit budgets	**Approach 2a:** Centralized funding Design funded by a corporate budget, distributed to business units through "corporate taxes"	**Approach 2b:** "Pay-to-play" funding Design funded through time-based agreements with internal and sometimes external clients; own P&L	**Approach 3:** Hybrid funding A "center of design excellence" funded by corporate budget; design otherwise funded through business unit budgets
Value orientation	**Design as business value driver** Design as core resource and integral part of the business units as a value contributor	**Design as corporate value driver** Design as core resource and corporate-wide value contributor	**Design as global service unit** Design as commodity-type resource; easily in- and outsourced	**Design as strategic value driver** Design as core resource; contributes value to organization as a whole and to individual business units
Resource allocation flexibility	**Limited:** annual design allocation Flexibility only within business unit that owns design resources	**Medium:** annual design allocation Some flexibility across business unit boundaries, based on short-term needs	**Medium–high:** project-based design allocation Resource allocation by project agreement; some flexibility across projects	**Limited–medium:** annual design allocation Some flexibility between business units and center of design excellence
Resource allocation decision making	Funding often historical and incremental; will depend on business unit growth priorities and realities	Funding often historical and incremental; will depend on company growth priorities and realities	Funding depends on demand generated by design leadership serving internal and external clients	Funding often historical and incremental; will depend on business unit and company growth priorities and realities
Effectiveness	Appropriate when design value is recognized by business unit leadership, and when support for design as a function has achieved critical mass	Appropriate during the incubation period, when design as a function has yet to demonstrate its value and develop its competencies	Appropriate when design is an established function, and has achieved critical mass and the maturity to compete with external design agencies	Appropriate when design function is a driver of strategic value for the organization; when a good balance of company and business unit priorities is possible

reporting lines that lead to design leadership as well, in the interest of maintaining standards of design excellence within the organization.[11] Among the organizational leaders we spoke with, those lines do not always exist. For example, the industrial designers at a consumer goods company follow a solid reporting line directly to their business unit manager and a dotted line to an R&D manager but do not report to the design leadership team at all. This means there is no design leader to oversee the designers' growth and career development, and nobody to champion the organizations' more global design objectives. This has now to be managed in good faith and collaboration between the leaders involved.

When designers report to the design leadership team, this lays part of the foundation for design excellence. Whether these reporting lines should be solid or dotted is a different question.

In one of the matrix-structured organizations in our sample, designers' efforts were funded by and entirely dedicated to their respective business units. The design leaders within the business units had dual reporting lines: a solid reporting line to the CDO, and a dotted line to their business unit leader. The rest of the designers had only one reporting line: a solid reporting line into design leadership. The CDO explained the decision to establish solid reporting lines into design leadership (instead of business leadership) by saying they wanted to "enable better design talent development, set relevant design objectives, to foster better design quality management, and drive brand compliance across business portfolios." The CDO went on to explain that dotted lines from design leaders to their business unit leaders were established to ensure effective calibration between business and design priorities and objectives. Even though design leadership was responsible for the career development of their designers, the decision to promote a designer (from senior design manager to design director, for example) always happened in consultation with the business unit leaders, because that promotion would be sponsored by the business unit in the end.

Despite the clear advantages, not many instances of the reporting structure described above were in place at the companies interviewed. Instead, when business units funded design, the relevant designers usually followed a solid reporting line to business unit leadership and a dotted line to design leadership.

In a matrix structure with dual-line reporting, tensions can crop up if everyone's priorities, goals, and day-to-day directives do not coincide. Direct reports may feel conflicted about whom they should take directives from and simply opt to manage up and ignore valid direction from dotted-line managers.[12] For design leaders to establish themselves as effective managers and make dual-line reporting work for their direct reports, they might wish to consider two collaboration approaches:[13]

- *Discuss and find balance:* Take the time to sit together — with the direct report and other manager(s) they report into — and align on goals and priorities, including how they contribute to wider organizational objectives. Doing so will create understanding for each other's roles and key concerns, which, in turn, opens the door to finding a balance of effective and transparent objectives for everyone concerned.

- *Look at objectives in new ways:* Sitting down to discuss and agree on priorities and goals often means reframing them to establish common ground. Everyone works for the same organization after all, so reaching agreement on objectives that transcend organizational silos should be motivating to every actor at the table.

Active dialogue between solid- and dotted-line business managers is an excellent way for the design leadership team to build strong collaborative relationships that support the design function. This may further embed design as a fundamental constituent of the organization. The goal is for everyone to jointly assume responsibility for the way opportunities and potential conflicts of interest are managed, and collaboratively pursue the organization's overarching strategic objectives. Ultimately, everybody at the organization in a way has a dotted line to each other; there is an ongoing need for trusted collaboration and mutual alignment in order to excel. It is counterproductive to approach reporting configurations as a play for power.

Table 4.2 presents an overview and some essential characteristics of the different design reporting lines we described here.

TABLE 4.2. Reporting line approaches for the design function.

Reporting Line	Single	Dual: Business/Design	Dual: Design/Business
Reporting approach	Solid reporting line to design	Solid reporting line to business unit; dotted to design	Solid reporting line to design; dotted to business unit
Objective setting & performance evaluation	Striving for design excellence Designers' priorities and objectives set and evaluated by design leadership	Striving for business excellence Designers' priorities and objectives set and evaluated by business unit leadership, aligned with design leadership	Striving for design excellence with business impact Designers' priorities and objectives set and evaluated by design leadership, aligned with business unit leadership
Career development	Career plan developed and enabled by design leadership	Career plan developed and enabled by business leadership, advice from design	Career plan developed and enabled by design leadership, advice from business
Potential challenges	Performance review is driven by design excellence; lack of alignment can isolate design from business realities	Performance review is driven by business excellence; aligning business and design leadership takes time	Performance review is driven by design excellence; aligning business and design leadership takes time

Reporting Lines of the Executive Design Leader

In our research, the heads of the design function, leading the organization's worldwide design efforts, typically operated at the VP level or higher. Only a small number of the executive design leaders interviewed reported with a solid or dotted line to the CEO. One VP of design operating in the computer industry said that their executive design leader followed a dotted line to the CEO. That VP made the observation that, given the small number of designers and the relative size of the design organization, the reporting structure was unusual:

> Having that reporting line to the CEO gives design access to power that we would not normally have, given the number of designers. It implies a very senior level of attention; we have a surprising amount of visibility.

The reason the executive design leader was reporting to the CEO was not because design had already been effectively scaled within the organization — it was because the company had the intent to scale design. CEOs limit the number of people that report to them, so it sends a very powerful message if design is doing so, even via a dotted line. This was corroborated by the head of design at a software firm, who said, "The fact that the company has the global head of design report to the CEO makes a statement about its importance and indicates the value the company places on design."

Being able to report to the CEO means having the opportunity to

- actively engage in dialogue on the strategic agenda of the company;
- share and receive feedback on the progress of the design function and its impact on the organization;
- address any topic that needs direct attention and follow up.

All of these serve the goal of successfully scaling design throughout the organization.

A direct line of reporting to the CEO would normally imply that an executive design leader is part of the executive board, and hence a member of the inner sanctum responsible for overall operational and strategic oversight.[14] It may, however, actually not be preferred by executive design leaders, as they may want to focus entirely on embedding design in the organization. This consideration was noted by the VP of design at an automotive company:

Design wants to be (and has to be) strategically recognized by top management — design should gain maximum exposure — but when design is part of the executive board, then of course as the executive design leader you have to sit in every board meeting and you have to work on things which are perhaps interesting in general, but not really the best use of your limited time as a design leader.

As indicated above, the majority of the executive design leaders we interviewed did not report to their CEO: they reported to one of the CEO's direct reports, or to an executive leader one level below the executive board. Who an executive design leader reports to can depend on how the organization has incorporated design into its operations — which further hints at the caliber of design's position and reach within the organization. For example, if leaders perceive design as contributing to the development of new innovations, the design leader may report to the chief technology officer or head of R&D; if design is expected to drive the organization's brand experiences, the design leader may report to the chief marketing or brand officer; when design works to optimize digital user experience, the design leader may report to the chief digital officer. Ideally, however, a chief marketing officer or chief technology officer should be a peer of the CDO, equally positioned in terms of reporting, rather than operating at a higher level in the hierarchy.

Table 4.3 summarizes the possible reporting approaches of the executive design leader and their advantages and disadvantages.

Another scenario is that the executive design leader has a solid-line reporting relationship with an executive leader responsible for a specific business unit or cluster of business units that all utilize design as a component

TABLE 4.3. Reporting line approaches for the executive design leader.

Reporting Line	Reports to the CEO	Reports to Function Leader	Reports to Business Leader
Description	Executive design leader reports via a solid or dotted reporting line to the CEO	Executive design leader reports to another functional leader who is part of the board of executive managers	Executive design leader reports to another business leader who is part of the board of executive managers
Value orientation	Design is seen as a core organizational competency	Design is seen as an integrated functional competency, instrumental to other functions	Design is seen as a core business competency, instrumental to business operations
Potential benefits	Direct access to CEO helps align design strategies; it signals design's strategic importance, which will facilitate design integration and scaling	Functional leader has greater design ownership thanks to functional affinity; design integrated into wider function enhances visibility and resource base	Business leader is potential advocate of the business value of design within the organization
Potential challenges	If design sits on the board of executive managers, much time will be devoted to nondesign issues; requires much business acumen	Design may not be perceived as equal to peer functions, or seen as a service rather than a strategy	Potential conflict of interest with companywide design objectives (such as brand compliance) versus objectives operating at the business level

of their operations. Conflicts of interest may arise with this type of reporting, however. If design as a whole is subsumed under the authority of a single business unit, the objectives of that business unit may demand higher priority, prevailing over those of other business units served equally by design, or over the objectives of the organization as a whole.

Most of the executive design leaders interviewed tended to follow a single, solid reporting line. Only in specific circumstances did some executive design leaders have one or two additional dotted-line relationships, depending on the scope of their activities and responsibilities.

LOCALIZING DESIGNERS

There are three basic localization configurations for in-house designers:

- *Approach 1: Distributed*: Designers' individual workspaces are spread out all over the organization. They sit in the same spaces as their business unit colleagues, separately from their design peers.
- *Approach 2: Partially co-located*: Designers' workspaces are spread out across the organization in different business units, but are co-located with other designers working for the same business unit in small studios.
- *Approach 3: Entirely co-located*: Designers working for units across the organization are predominantly seated together in a dedicated design center.

Design workspace localization is often tied to the organization's sponsorship approach, but not always. Even if sponsorship is decentralized, and design is funded by individual business units, the in-house design team may still physically sit together in a centrally located design center or studio — as was the case in some of the organizations we consulted. What follows now is a closer look at the pros and cons of these three approaches.[15]

Approach 1: Distributed

In this approach, designers physically sit within a specific business unit for which they work. They are members of a multifunctional team responsible for specific products, brands, or markets. One organization we interviewed had situated designers' workspaces together with representatives from other departments in what they had named "brand hubs" — physical spaces designed to facilitate brand immersion. A variation of this model is when designers work on a specific project and physically sit with their multifunctional project team cohort in a dedicated area. The project might be bookended, for example to develop new product features, and once the project ends the designers are allocated to another project team and, accordingly, physically located in the same area as this new project team. Or the project team might be permanent and the project an open-ended one, such as managing the continuous improvement of a certain key milestone in a customer journey.

Atlassian, a software company with Australian origins, seats its multifunctional innovation teams together in dedicated spaces. The team members come from three core areas of software development: engineering, project management, and design. These three areas of expertise share team leadership responsibilities and accountability — the company calls this team formation a "triad" — so that everyone's efforts and priorities are in line, and an effective balance between satisfying business, customer, and technology demands can be maintained.[16]

Another well-known example of a software company locating multifunctional teams in dedicated spaces is Spotify. Each one — known as a "squad" — is relatively small. They share a space, operate relatively autonomously, and fulfill specific missions. The overarching aim of this team structure is to speed up software development.[17] Teams that are responsible for product features have a ratio of about seven engineers to every one designer (and one product manager). One Spotify design director responsible for user experience explained that this approach had led to the designers feeling isolated, which negatively affected the quality of their work. So this design leader adjusted the seating arrangements slightly, allowing designers from a few different teams to sit near each other — creating a kind of mini design hub — in areas fairly close to their squad mates. According to the design director, the results were enhanced collaboration and improved team outcomes.[18]

A major advantage of this approach — being fully embedded within the team and also actually being physically co-located together — is that what designers actually do and how they contribute to outcomes becomes more visible to nondesigners. One professional services organization adopted a new organizational model that includes co-locating designers together with the other members of the multifunctional project team. The design director remarked on the difference it made when compared to the prior approach, in which designers were not co-located and worked separately from the rest of the team:

> What we as designers did, and how we contributed to successful outcomes, was often invisible when the old framework was in place. We were isolated and anonymized. That's why we love the new horizontal framework . . . the contributions we make surface much better. In the old framework, it almost was like offshoring labor a little. On the receiving end, it was like, "I don't know how [things are done] and I don't really care."

Sitting designers together with other team members paves the way to them being recognized as integral members of the team. A framework under which designers are contracted in for a short period — maybe two weeks — to deliver certain results to the project team does not make it possible for design to become a true strategic partner. When designers are co-located, there is a better understanding of what design does, and that understanding creates a deeper sense of empathy and mutual respect over time, which can mean that eventual implementation of designerly ideas and approaches may also go more smoothly. As one CDO at a computer hardware manufacturer so eloquently put it,

> The project team members are vested in making decisions that keep the design integrity purer, versus diluting it with "death by a thousand cuts" — "We didn't really understand why you did that, so we just changed it to this."

The benefit goes both ways, of course. Working together with staff from other departments and business units on a day-to-day basis helps designers to better understand and empathize with the perspectives, goals, and approaches taken by other departments and units, which in turn makes collaboration easier and will likely result in improved outcomes generated more rapidly.

While there are clear benefits to physically locating designers within multifunctional project teams, a challenge also emerges. How can a design culture, a coherent design language, and consistent brand experiences emerge when designers are not sitting together? This conundrum was expressed by the VP of design at an automotive supplier, whose designers are located in various R&D centers spread out all over the organization:

> We are very much scattered across the world, which means we have to compensate for the fact that we are not all under one roof. It's more difficult to nurture a strong, common design culture.

This issue can be resolved through design management activities such as having frequent virtual design critique sessions.

When designers are massively outnumbered by one or more subgroups within a business unit, or at the project level by other collaborators, they sometimes feel pressured to conform to the concerns of others, and may be unable to maintain design-related priorities. As a former VP of design at Twitter suggested,

> Designers in product teams are vulnerable to "path of least resistance" behavior — engineers will ask the designer to make things simpler so implementation is easier. You're accountable to a different set of values when you're working with other designers.[19]

Indeed, the size of the design team may determine whether designers work in separate business units or together. For example, the aforementioned computer hardware CDO initially wanted to build critical mass in the number of in-house designers employed within the organization, and establish a certain design culture, before dispersing the designers. "Now we've gotten to the point where we have healthy critical mass; we're breaking up the design teams and embedding them closer to each business group."

Approach 2: Partially Co-Located

Here, designers' physical workspaces are located in the same general physical areas as the business units they work for, or very close by, but occupy a specifically designated design space. Their efforts are wholly dedicated to the business unit that sponsors them (or units, if more than one). A major benefit of this model is that it replicates (on a smaller scale) the atmosphere of a real design studio. The studio setting facilitates interaction among the designers as peers. They often share similar passions and objectives, and will help each other execute and advance the design craft to the best of their abilities. Being physically located within or close to the sponsoring unit also facilitates the incorporation of wider priorities; this design proximity can also encourage effective use of design as a strategic competency.

A possible disadvantage of seating designers together, but in separate design centers or studios, is that it may lead to various design hive minds that diverge in terms of culture and process across the design organization. As a result, the delivery of customer experiences may diverge as well, having a negative impact on design consistency. For this framework to serve the overarching aims of design, explicit design coordination and alignment mechanisms must be put in place — coordination and cooperation will not arise organically, as they would in studio-like environments.

Approach 3: Entirely Co-Located

In the third location approach, the majority of designers are physically located in a single dedicated design center. This is normally the case when design is sponsored by the corporate budget, but it may also be adopted when designers are covered by funds from several business units combined.

In addition to this main design center (design's headquarters), there may be a few well-connected satellite design studios in other geographic locations to serve major clients or markets in those locations as and when needed.

Where to locate the main design center is a strategic decision that requires careful deliberation. There are essentially two options: at the headquarters of the organization, or in an inspiring location that may or may not be geographically close to the organization's headquarters.

A major benefit of placing the main design center at the company's headquarters is the proximity it would have to organizational leadership — to the strategic heart of the organization, as it were. Residing at the headquarters sends a signal to the rest of the organization that design is integral to organizational strategy. Designers operate in plain sight visible to other key stakeholders, which may serve to further embed design inside the organization. For example, a business manager from a health company was somewhat critical that their main design center was located in a vibrant nearby city rather than at the somewhat remote headquarters:

> Design people are often seen as a different species. And sitting in a different location, away from where all the other folks sit, far away from the business, has created further disparity among us.

Having the main design center located at the headquarters rather than "away from where all the other folks sit" may facilitate the recognition of design as a valuable resource and also help ground design within the organization. It invites designers to look beyond their design perspectives, as indicated by some of the design leaders interviewed. However, if a company's headquarters is located in a geographic area that is not very inspiring and/or is relatively remote, it may be more difficult to attract design talent. In some instances, organizations do both: the majority of designers are located in a design center at the organization's headquarters, but there are also one or more satellite design studios in big, vibrant cities, precisely to attract design talent. According to the CDO of a furniture company whose localization approach was similar,

> More than half our designers are located in our headquarters in [a relatively rural area]. We also have a satellite design office in [a big city] which allows us to tap into a design talent pool that is deeper and, in some ways, richer than what we can find in [the relatively rural area]. But it's not that those designers then function separately from the rest of us. Internally, we sometimes use the mantra "two locations, one team." It's not two different teams in two different locations.

A major advantage of localizing the majority of design staff in the same physical location is that it optimizes opportunities for peer-to-peer learning and cross-fertilization among them. It can help designers grow in their craft more quickly. It also creates the conditions for creative buzz to emerge and fosters the development of the "connective tissue" between designers that is beneficial for motivation and inspiration. Aligning creative expression and consistency is so much easier when all the design disciplines sit together. In the words of the furniture company CDO quoted earlier in the chapter, their designers are co-located in one creative space because this allows the designers to

> [l]earn from each other and be able to quickly leverage work that's been done in different parts of the business, which will build consistency where helpful or, at the very least, creates awareness of other work that is happening; it also creates a spirit of camaraderie, which is important as well.

When designers are not physically scattered across the organization, design can more readily make itself known and more clearly position itself as a consolidated creative powerhouse. In addition, working from a single location may ultimately shield designers from unnecessary distractions, particularly if the design center has a restricted entry policy. Co-locating designers at a central studio or center carves out a secure space for creativity — designers have room to breathe; they can explore, make mistakes, learn, be curious, and seamlessly collaborate. The act of creativity is an act of vulnerability that requires a supportive environment to flourish. A single shared design space also means investments in equipment, tools, and other physical resources — to support materials labs and maker spaces, for example — is more cost effective, because there are more designers using the same equipment.

A point of attention when creating a separate design center is that in addition to potentially creating a physical barrier between the businesses or the wider organization and the designers, it might also create a mental one. This may hinder cross-departmental collaboration, which in turn can have a negative impact on how design is scaled across the organization.

As noted by the head of design from a professional services organization, a design leader should make sure that their design center is not seen by the rest of the organization as a "cool kids club, with Eames chairs, and turtlenecks, and glass walls," that does nothing to actually move the needle from an organizational perspective. Any type of negative impression could severely hamper the reach of design inside the organization as a whole. When considerable corporate funds are invested in building a "very cool design space," if the design leader is not able to effectively and convincingly demonstrate how design drives performance, resentment within the organization may grow, which would make the task of convincing leaders to embrace design more difficult.

A summary of localizing frameworks and their implications is provided in Table 4.4.

TABLE 4.4. Localization approaches and their characteristics.

Physical Location	Distributed	Partially Co-Located	Entirely Co-Located
Description	Designers physically located with business unit colleagues as part of multifunctional project teams	Designers located with or close to their business unit colleagues, seated together in a dedicated design area	Designers all seated together in a dedicated design center, regardless of business unit or design discipline
Design community connection	Isolated from design peers, disconnected from learning and growing design competencies	Connection among small group of peers enabling some learning; need to create one team mentality across multiple locations	The close connection among design peers fosters a strong design culture; design more visible as a community
Design integration	**High integration at the project level** Fluid communication among various functional disciplines facilitates integration of diverse perspectives	**High integration at the business level** Fluid communication between business and design facilitates integration of business priorities	**High integration at the functional level** Fluid communication among various design disciplines facilitates design consistency
Potential challenges	**"No design clout"** Due to lack of critical mass, design perspectives may be overwhelmed by technology or business perspectives	**"Together, but separate"** Less attuned to design perspectives as business perspective dominates; lack of alignment with other design hubs	**"Us vs. them"** Design might appear as an ivory tower; the design function may be less attuned to the business perspective

Deployment

Once the organizational framework for design has been drafted it must be endorsed by the organization's executive board. To obtain the approval of the board, the executive design leader must have a clear rationale behind the framework and how, overall, it will support the company's strategic goals and priorities. The structured approach described at the start of the chapter will help design executives provide a compelling case.

Getting the board to endorse the organizational framework is only the beginning. The executive design leader must then make sure that the framework is adopted throughout the organization. Ensuring that the organizational framework for design is properly deployed is of particular importance if the organization has a matrix management structure, in which decision making is more decentralized. There are four tactics that may streamline the wider deployment process:

- *Extensively discuss working drafts of the proposed framework.* Discussions with relevant organizational stakeholders facilitate the socialization process. These discussions must take place before the final draft of the framework is produced and shared with the executive board for acceptance and endorsement, so that any relevant alterations can be incorporated.
- *Engage in effective communication.* Once the executive board has endorsed the new (or revised) design organizational framework, they could distribute an official memo to announce the agreed-upon framework and signal their endorsement to every level of the organization.
- *Prepare easy-to-read, short documents.* Condense the essential components of the framework into an easy-to-read, short document for managers, using the appropriate content, language, and register for these audiences. Clearly explain the rationale for changes in current practices and/or the addition of new practices. Be transparent about "what's in it for the organization" in terms of the value the framework offers, and the implications it carries for the departments or units and the wider organization.

- *Use phased implementation.* The best approach to securing organizationwide acceptance of the framework might be for the executive design leader to stage a phased implementation. Every single component of the framework does not necessarily need to be implemented with the same priority; to facilitate acceptance and ensure successful uptake, a step-by-step approach might be wiser. For example, if the organizational framework designates business unit sponsorship of design, and physically localizes designers close to their business unit colleagues, it may more effective to assess, case by case, whether the time is right to actually implement the framework. It may be better to wait until the number of designers to be placed within the business unit has reached a certain threshold to guarantee the presence of a certain "design clout."

CONCLUSION

To draft and implement an effective organizational framework, design leadership must make consequential choices related to budget sponsorship, reporting lines, and staff localization. The final constellation of these aspects should support present and future excellence in design.

When defining and implementing an organizational framework for design at your organization, different dualities will arise that must be harmonized and balanced. We summarize some of the most salient here.

Decentralized Versus Centralized Funding

The basic duality to manage here is the degree to which design should be sponsored centrally by the organization or distributed across individual business units. It is a decision that influences (and is influenced by) how design is prioritized within the organization. When design is sponsored in a decentralized fashion, its focus will particularly be on driving business excellence; when it is sponsored in a centralized fashion, its focus will be more on obtaining design excellence overall.

Formal Authority Versus Informal Influence

Design leadership needs to make decisions about accountability and control. Who will have the formal authority to influence, define, and champion design horizons? The answer to this involves mechanisms of direct control: the structure of reporting lines, for example, determines who is in the position to drive priorities and objectives. However, influence itself, particularly in a matrix structure, also depends on the degree to which design leadership has established trusting relationships with business leaders. These trusting relationships are not a given; they often require a demonstration of expertise and thought leadership. Trust, though elusive, is extremely valuable, because relationships built on it facilitate calibration among leaders and create openings for indirect influence on priorities and objectives.

Co-Location of Design Versus Distribution of Design

When deciding where designers will sit, and in which configurations, an important duality to weigh relates to striving for co-location of design versus distribution of design. Should designers be distributed across multifunctional project teams and separated from their design peers or should designers be co-located together in dedicated design centers and separated from other areas of activity? Distribution of designers across multifunctional teams facilitates alignment across the different areas of activity; co-location in dedicated design centers facilitates calibration among designers.

To effectively navigate and respond to these dualities, design leadership has to constellate its governance to suit its specific organizational context. It is impossible to provide the ultimate blueprint for how this should look, given that every context is different. However, when a matrix structure is present, the following constellation may provide the latitude and grounding for both business and design excellence to flourish:

- Under hybrid design sponsoring, the majority of design costs are sponsored by business units and a small portion is funded on the corporate level, to support a center of design excellence. Decentralized sponsoring by business units may signal recognition of design as a valuable tool to enhance business growth and may facilitate the scaling of design; centralized sponsoring on the other hand will guarantee corporatewide design consistency and compliance.

- Designers follow a single, solid reporting line to design leadership. Reporting to design leadership will support designers' careers, professional development, and day-to-day design activities, given design leaders' knowledge and expertise. One solid reporting line, instead of dual reporting lines, will create clarity about who is the manager and is setting the objectives.
- Design leadership follows dual reporting lines. The executive design leader would report with a dotted line to the CEO; this indirect reporting puts design on the strategic agenda and signals the strategic importance of design to the organization. Having a solid reporting line into the CEO may not be justified from a numbers perspective. It may also distract from design-related matters if a design leader is asked to attend to other corporate matters as well. Design leaders who are dedicated to specific business units would report with a dotted line to business unit leaders and a solid line to the executive design leader. Dual reporting will guarantee a balance between business and design priorities and goals.
- Designers are co-located at a central design center with design hubs across businesses or regions. The majority of designers would largely be localized at a single, dedicated design center at company headquarters. Having a center will cultivate design consistency, nurture a design community, and bring design closer to the rest of the organization. Small design hubs may be created to better serve local markets or regions.

Drafting and implementing an effective organizational framework for design is a challenging task for design leadership that requires knowledge of operations, finance, and HR management. The organizational framework will form the foundation and establish the rules for engagement that are needed to effectively scale design throughout the organization.

PART 2

Empowering the Design Team

CHAPTER 5

Design Taxonomy

The design taxonomy defines what to expect from designers in terms of specific competencies and roles. It transparently outlines the boundaries of the design function within the organization and enables clarity when working in cross-functional teams.

THE DESIGN TAXONOMY is a clear and formalized description of the design function in terms of scope, roles, competencies, and seniorities. By defining core team roles and the key competencies needed to reach design excellence, the taxonomy will empower the design team members to effectively collaborate with each other and the organization at large. A formalized and well-communicated taxonomy will enable the executive design leader to build and scale the design function and share with the rest of the company the tasks, responsibilities, and variety of competencies present in the design function. Finally, design talent is central to the success of the design function and to its ability to generate value for a company. Creating, growing, and demonstrably adhering to the function's taxonomy is fundamental to attract and keep top talent by offering them a transparent and attractive career path.

This chapter covers the core elements of a design taxonomy, and how to create one. It begins by identifying the activities that are central to creating a design taxonomy, and then moves on to defining the scope of design and providing some guidelines for how to identify the contours of that scope.

The following sections are dedicated to clarifying some key design roles and competencies that the design taxonomy might include, and explaining how those competencies can be combined into a hierarchy of job levels. That hierarchy helps determine the career trajectories the design function will offer. After that, what goes into the making of a CDO, and some variations of the CDO job title, are explored. The conclusion presents some dualities that an executive design leader must manage when developing and deploying the design taxonomy, and provides some guidelines on how to excel at creating what will eventually become a cornerstone of design function excellence.

DEVELOPING A DESIGN TAXONOMY

To construct a taxonomy, executive design leaders should start by collecting information on the following:

- *Industry-specific insights*: to learn about the scope of design and how the design team is created and developed in other companies as a potential benchmark
- *The human resource (HR) policies and processes*: to set the boundary conditions for the design taxonomy such as compensation structures, job levels, job title architectures, job descriptions, and career development approaches
- *The taxonomies of other functions within the organization*: for comparison, alignment, and learning; the components of these taxonomies might not necessarily match design requirements precisely, but conceptually, they can be good reference points
- *Status of the design function*: to understand where the design function currently stands in terms of its scope, the key roles that designers play, and the core competencies they fulfill
- *Company values and desired behaviors*: to guide the formulation of design-specific behaviors to be used in the recruitment of design talent

Once this information has been gathered, the executive design leader can start to develop the taxonomy that best suits the design direction and strategy for excellence. It should include a definition of the design scope, an overview of key design roles and related competencies, and a job framework replete with descriptions of the different job levels.

The taxonomy should be developed on the basis of a preferred state of design excellence: one that appropriately positions design inside the organization and anticipates a future scaling strategy. That future state, and not only the current size and composition of the design team, should always be in the executive design leader's mind when setting up a taxonomy. If the design function has not reached a sufficient level of maturity within the organization, a sophisticated taxonomy may look (to other stakeholders and to executive leaders) a little like overkill. Nevertheless, a well-defined, forward-looking taxonomy is more likely futureproof — it might require some alignment at the beginning but it will not have to be adapted too often along the way.

One important way to facilitate corporate endorsement of the taxonomy is to develop it in close collaboration with HR. Working in tandem with HR is a good way to create awareness about the character and competencies of the design function, and an opportunity to initiate the kind of relationship that will lead to partnership between them. Partnering with HR will ensure that design taxonomy components line up with the guiding principles used by other functions in the company, which will make comparison, formalization, and implementation easier. However, these guiding principles are generally based on job classifications and evaluation systems that cater mostly to managerial contexts and will need to be adapted to the specificities of developing a taxonomy for creative professionals. For example, many companies develop internal taxonomies based on the Hay system,[1] which does not capture the nature of design roles because it uses traditional business evaluation criteria such as profit and loss (P&L) responsibilities, number of reports, size of organization, and revenue as benchmarks. Design executives, on the other hand, might require employees to deliver results relative to creative leadership, budget management, and thought leadership. Given these differences, the executive design leader should lead the discussion on how to adapt HR taxonomy guidelines to the scope, responsibilities, and key competencies of the design function.

Another way to facilitate a widespread acceptance of the taxonomy is to socialize it with other functional leaders to discuss where design might fit into their activities and how design might collaborate with them. Executive design leaders can run these discussions by comparing their taxonomy with those of other functions. In this way they can not only ward off misunderstandings about the role of design but also realize that sometimes other functions' existing taxonomies lack detail or comprehensiveness in defining their scope and their staff's roles and competencies, which might represent an unexpected but fundamental roadblock to effective collaboration. More specifically, other functions' difficulties in understanding the role of design might be due to a lack of definition on their own scope of activities. In these cases, a good approach to follow could be to start a collaborative dialogue with the other functional leaders aimed at aligning and clarifying reciprocal taxonomies to overcome unclarities and potential overlaps.

THE SCOPE OF DESIGN

The first step in building a design taxonomy is defining the scope of the design function: the range of activities that the design function will perform for the organization. Defining the scope of the design function means indicating where design can add value to the company, in general and in relation to other functions in the organization — for example, marketing and R&D.

Furthermore, the scope of the design activities clarifies which competencies should be part of the design function, and thus which professionals should be hired. These benchmarks enable the design leader to define which design specializations must come under the umbrella of the design function and which can be elsewhere. That information can be used to create and promote a shared understanding of design within the organization, and deliver high-quality design outcomes.

The research conducted for this book indicates that design specializations inside large organizations are typically product or industrial design, user experience (UX) or interaction design, graphic design, brand design, and user research. In addition, several new specializations are gaining traction — strategic design and data-driven design, for example — a development that reflects the evolution of design as a field. Other, more context-specific design specializations — packaging design or retail design in marketing-driven organizations, for example — might have their place in the taxonomy as required. Some executive design leaders prefer to outsource highly specialized design talent. As the design leader at one technology company recalled, the design team would have been much larger if it had incorporated designers specialized in downstream, "repetitive" design activities such as "marketing collateral, model making, and desktop publishing." However, the decision to exclude these was a conscious one for that leader, in line with their definition of the scope of the design function.

The starting point for defining the scope of design is the mandate that the design leader agrees upon with the executive team when hired. That mandate will not necessarily reflect the full potential of the design function, as some organizations do not recognize the value of design from the start. It is up to executive design leaders to define a broader scope, and then direct their efforts towards achieving it with the means, both present and future, at their disposal.

Design leaders should be thoughtful and realistic about the territory they seek to claim when defining the scope of design. Carefully consider which domains are the responsibility of other functions; use the taxonomies of other relevant functions for reference to prevent the unnecessary perception that the design taxonomy overlaps too broadly. In organizations with an R&D culture, for example, the scope of the design function as it relates to innovation must be thoughtfully considered. And in organizations with a marketing culture, design's relationship to branding activities will require close alignment. By using their ability to build bridges, design leaders emphasize complementarities when overlaps with the domains of other functions emerge. As an example, the VP of global design of a PC hardware manufacturer indicated that when it came to defining the scope of design within overall corporate innovation strategy, the focus was on "a space that hadn't really progressed and evolved in a very long time: bringing modern experiences and modern relevancy to the way people use and engage with technology."

As explained in Chapter 1, "Design Context," the design scope can include different value areas, such as innovation, branding, customer engagement, or efficiency. The contours of the design scope will change, however, as a consequence of changes in organizational dynamics — due to restructuring or the arrival of new senior management, for example — and as design evolves as a discipline. The CDO of a home appliances company took note of the dynamism that characterizes the definition of scope:

What should design be doing, in a firm like ours? What is design doing in other, similar types of industries, firms? Where should it be going? Because design is sort of this moving target now for me, it extends from style to consumer experience to digital to business . . . to everything.

Executive design leaders should regularly review and eventually adjust their definition of the design scope and then update their design taxonomies accordingly.

KEY ROLES TO INCLUDE IN DESIGN TAXONOMIES

Once the design scope has been defined, the executive design leader should create an overview of all the roles and competencies that the design function will need to deliver value.

A design taxonomy should define four key roles:

1. *Design management (strategizing, relationship management, value identification)*: Design management directs the efforts of the design function; manages the design team; and aligns design with business objectives, strategies, and processes. Designers in this role interact with other business unit and functional leaders to capture and stretch their needs, and translate them into related design objectives and activities. Designers in this role should enable the delivery of design outcomes. This will ensure that business units and departments understand and appreciate design competencies, embrace the work of designers, and take design objectives into account. Design managers must guide the attainment of design objectives, so that the design function keeps generating value for the company.

2. *Creative direction (design quality, competency development, value creation)*: Creative direction focuses on the craft of design and on ensuring consistent and appropriate quality across design outcomes — for example, in terms of aesthetics, human factors, user experiences, brand manifestations. How quality standards are defined depends on the stated design direction (especially its principles) and the company's business goals and competitive context. Designers in this role also follow current developments in the field to keep the organization's design practices up to date.

3. *Design research (insight and foresight)*: Design research generates relevant user insights and explores future opportunities related to new and

potentially disruptive technologies, new markets, and emerging socio-cultural trends. The core goal of this role is to identify sources of innovation, either in technology or branding, and bring those into the design function and the company.

4. *Design operations (efficiency and compliance)*: Operations management drives the efficiency and effectiveness of the design process. This includes project management, managing outsourced relationships (including administrative aspects), ensuring compliance and consistency of output in design processes, and integrating the design team's workflow into the company's wider development context. Rapid delivery and cost control are important objectives for design professionals working in this role.

Design taxonomy roles are different and complementary, with interrelated priorities and drivers. Differing drivers can create tension: a creative director focuses more on quality and relevancy, and less on cost restrictions and development time, for example, which are the core drivers of a design operations manager. While such tension can stimulate healthy debate and even lead to innovative solutions, the design leader should make sure that contrasting interests are balanced to the benefit of the overall goals of the design function and, ultimately, of the organization. The role of the (executive) design leadership team is to manage a smooth collaboration among the various roles and make sure that each role and staff member receives equal attention and equal opportunities for growth.

The range of design specializations defined in the scope are usually present within most roles, with some adaptations determined by the specific context of a role. The type of designers hired for design management roles depends on the type of company. In product-driven contexts, managerial roles within the design function are usually covered by product or industrial designers. In service-driven companies, design leaders tend to be UX or service designers. The creative direction team should have representatives from every design specialization; achieving quality in design outcomes requires the contribution of all kinds of designers. Design research benefits from skilled conceptual thinkers having a mix of backgrounds and expertise, different design and research specializations, and also other, nondesign backgrounds. That is why it is relatively common to invite professionals with backgrounds in sociology, anthropology, psychology, or the relevant natural sciences, and even artists, to occupy design research roles. Design operations positions can also be offered to professionals from different backgrounds, such as project management or manufacturing, mostly if they have experience in the creative industry.

SUPPORTING KEY ROLES: DESIGN COMPETENCIES

While designers from any specialization could perform the four key roles described in the previous section, each role calls for a distinct set of specific competencies. Identifying the core competencies that belong to the different roles is a key part of creating a good taxonomy. A competency is a combination of knowledge, behaviors, and skills that gives someone the potential to execute a task effectively.[2] Any competency can be translated into a set of observable behaviors that an individual should demonstrate when that specific competency is owned.

Each role requires a combination of core design competencies and other "soft" competencies.[3] For instance, the head of design of an e-commerce company explained,

> As a web designer, you are certainly expected to be proficient at designing wireframes. But you also need to be skilled at collaboration and teamwork. You are expected to collaborate with different stakeholders and partners. You may not have exposure to senior-level people — and that's fine — but within your squad, you must be active contributors and support the team.

Following are examples of competencies that are specific to each key design role.[4]

1. Design management (strategizing, relationship management, value identification)

- *Relationship building:* Establish and cultivate good working relationships with multiple functions in the business to encourage and facilitate design collaboration. Work in collaboration with designers, business managers, and executives to maximize value generated by design.

- *Strategic mindset*: Proactively promote and demonstrate the strategic value of design and connect design to business opportunities. Focus on identifying high business value opportunities for growth and create strategies for competitive advantage.
- *Business acumen*: Speak the language of business and design, be comfortable translating business challenges into appropriate design programs, and share design outcomes in relevant ways with business leadership to maximize the impact of design investments.

2. Creative direction (design quality, competency development, value creation)

- *Design craft*: Be familiar with design tools and methods and apply these according to high standards. Be a design purist with internalized standards to gauge aesthetic quality and style; be driven to deliver unique customer solutions.
- *Creative leadership*: Inspire creativity; lead by example. Develop and share creative vision and make the imaginary real through powerful storytelling. Promote inclusiveness and diversity; use design mentorship as a team enabler.
- *Brand design quality*: Lead the creation of high-quality, meaningful brand experiences across all touchpoints based on a clear vision. Capture the brand experience ecosystem to create holistic customer solutions.

3. Design research (insight and foresight)

- *Research expertise*: Gather insights and conduct foresight activities by combining a wide variety of research methods and tools. Remain sensitive to technological trends and new market developments.
- *Research outcomes translation*: Make insight and foresight data relevant by connecting them to design actions and business objectives. Use storyboards and inspiring communication tools to facilitate research-driven decision making.

- *Imagineering*: Use the imagination to connect business and design research insights in unexpected ways to inspire new value spaces, future scenarios, and investment prioritization.

4. Design operations (efficiency and compliance)

- *Project management*: Manage activities, timing, budgets, and resources for a project; understand and implement different project management approaches (for example, cascade, agile).
- *Processes management*: Continuously evaluate processes and initiate improvements in workflow; drive value optimization and design quality simultaneously. Appropriate process ownership and leadership lead to end-to-end optimization and business advantages such as manufacturing time-to-market, efficiency, and design consistency.
- *Supplier management*: Build strategic relationships with suppliers to optimize supply chain management for design production. Understand the manufacturing environment and sourcing to drive supplier rationales, process optimization, and business value.

Holders of these competencies will have different levels of sophistication (such as fundamental, experienced, specialist, master). Competency levels translate into progressive levels of professional development, and their transparent communication reveals how internal designers can advance in their design careers. The CDO of a home appliances manufacturer, for example, suggested that leadership competency can begin with a supportive and proactive attitude during a project, and then grow into leading a small project, then leading a complex project involving stakeholders from other functions, and finally coaching of others in leadership skills by doing projects together.

Table 5.1 summarizes how the key roles, competencies, and levels per competency are built up into a comprehensive framework. As suggested by the empty columns and row, the number of competencies required to fill a role and the level of sophistication per competency might vary depending on the company and the scope and maturity of design. Furthermore, the

TABLE 5.1. Competency framework for key design roles.

		Key role A **Design Management** strategizing/ relationship management/ value identification				Key role B **Creative Direction** quality/competency development/value creation				Key role C **Design Research** insight/foresight				Key role D **Design Operations** efficiency/compliance			
		Competency 1	Competency 2	Competency 3		Competency 1	Competency 2	Competency 3		Competency 1	Competency 2	Competency 3		Competency 1	Competency 2	Competency 3	
Competency Levels	Level A Fundamental																
	Level B Experienced																
	Level C Specialist																
	Level D Master																
	—																

number of competencies and sophistication might expand as the design function enters new value areas over time, or as the expertise of internal designers increases.

In addition to specific competencies for the different design roles, some taxonomies also include cultural behaviors that the global design team is expected to adhere to as they go about their daily activities. The goal of defining these behaviors and including them in the taxonomy is to create and consolidate a shared design culture. The cultural behaviors are generally aligned with the design principles and should guide designers' behavior when interacting with other stakeholders, during meetings with clients, and during onboarding, for example — not only when engaged in their core tasks. Desirable design culture behaviors are the same across all design roles and aligned with the company values or preferred behaviors. They might fix a standard level of a particular capacity that the design function expects from all its staff. For example, even if business acumen is a competency that designers playing a design management role must have, the culture might demand a general level of business acumen that all designers should demonstrate.

SHAPING A CAREER FRAMEWORK FOR DESIGNERS

By growing their skills, experience, and competencies, designers can progress in their careers. The possibilities and requirements for career advancement should be transparent and well communicated, so that designers can take ownership of their career trajectories. A useful tool to provide them is the job framework: an overview of all job levels (and titles) across key design roles. The framework describes jobs and job levels in terms of combinations of competency levels needed for a key design role. A longer career will likely come with more advanced levels of competency.

Job levels within the design function usually range from (junior) designer to senior designer, lead designer, design manager or principal, design director, design executive (VP, SVP, CDO). How many levels there are depends on the size of the organization, and should reflect the customs established by other functions in the company — the salary grades and career paths in design should match those of employees in other functions. For instance, in some companies, executive positions are roles directly appointed and regulated by the executive board. In that case, the executive level could be limited to the design management area and/or not managed by the executive design leader. In addition, the number of job levels depends on the kinds of growth and career flexibility the organization needs, which is related to the overall size of the design function, the size of the organization, and the need to differentiate roles. When executive design leaders are in the early stages of their scaling efforts, it is possible that not all the design roles are installed and that the job levels within some roles only reach the manager or director level for the time being.

A clear and transparent job framework has many uses. Designers can use it as a self-evaluation and motivational tool to progress in their career. By clearly knowing what is expected to make higher or lateral job moves, designers can plan their careers, adjust their efforts, and have open and constructive training and coaching-related discussions during their performance meetings. (More on how to evaluate and recognize the performance of designers can be found in Chapter 6, "Design Resources"). An explicit job framework helps design leaders recruit new talent, because it reveals competency gaps and allows leaders to quickly create consistent job templates to attract the right candidates. A job framework that is aligned with the design jobs and career paths of other companies will help retain design talent, as designers will perceive that they are offered growth opportunities that are commensurate with what other companies are offering — especially other firms that have a reputation for design excellence. When job frameworks are based on benchmark information, in line with other functions, they create comparable references in terms of career opportunities and salaries for the various design roles. Finally, as for the whole taxonomy, a well-defined job framework demonstrates the maturity and professionalization of the design function, facilitating the development of robust relationships with the other functions and business units.

From the research interviews it emerged that offering dual career opportunities — that is, offering designers the possibility to choose a growth path either in managerial roles or as experts in their discipline — is highly desired. Given their creative nature and passion for their craft, some designers might not be excited by or interested in managerial and executive roles. In traditional career ladders, these designers would have limited opportunities for growth and responsibility other than going into managerial roles. Often, designers who are passionate about the design craft prefer to develop their career as independent professionals or in more creative design agencies. To accommodate and retain this kind of talent and offer them growth opportunities, executive design leaders create dual career paths as part of their career framework: one for designers to take on managerial roles, and one comparable and equally rewarding for those designers who want to keep growing as experts in their design discipline. This second path leads to the job title of design principal (also referred to as master designer or design fellow in some companies), and starts after designers have completed a few steps in the career ladder that are the same for every designer (usually after becoming senior designer). The VP of design at an automotive company explained how the different paths play out in that company:

> On one side there is a more managerial career path, where you would eventually lead a function globally, such as color and trim function, advanced design function, user experience, or overall design function leader, or you would lead a design studio in one of the regions and be hierarchically responsible for the people. That would

be the managerial career path. On the other side, you can go down the expert path, like the principal designer path, where you would become a sort of design guru — not necessarily managing people, but being able to manage huge projects around your area of expertise, including very complex customer technologies.

Design principals generally are recognized by their peers as thought leaders in their specific area of expertise. For instance, they are frequently invited to be keynote speakers at conferences and to publish white papers in their area of expertise, are often very active and available on social media, have thought-provoking dialogues with their peers, and are invited to sit on the juries of design awards related to their specializations. Design principals also have mentorship responsibilities within the design team in relation to their area of expertise. While the design principal role (or similar roles) is offered to provide opportunities for growth for those who wish to excel in their field of design expertise rather than engage in management, the role still may involve some managerial activities and require managerial competencies. In the words of the design director at a consumer goods manufacturer,

Design principals need to have some basic managerial skills — time management and project management, for example — to be able to operate within the collaborative environment that characterizes the design function and earn the trust of other team members.

The design principal role is, in general, a role in which designers operate at the manager level. It seems less common (at the moment of this writing) for designers to be offered the opportunity to excel as an expert while operating at the executive level. One notable exception is at IBM. In addition to the design principal role, IBM created the role of distinguished designer as a further step in the design thought leadership career ladder.[5] This position acknowledges exemplary design expertise and gives the designers holding it a leadership role in further developing certain design practices within the design function and the company in general. Distinguished designers belong to the executive team of their business

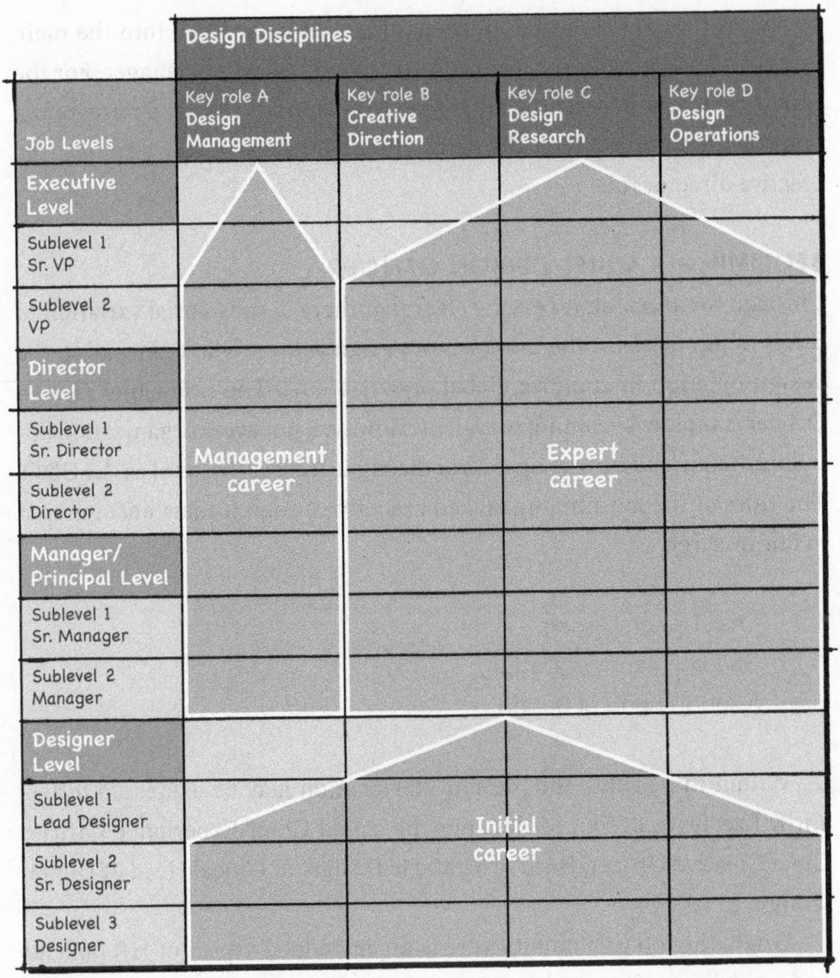

Job Levels	Key role A Design Management	Key role B Creative Direction	Key role C Design Research	Key role D Design Operations
Design Disciplines				
Executive Level				
Sublevel 1 Sr. VP				
Sublevel 2 VP				
Director Level		Management career		Expert career
Sublevel 1 Sr. Director				
Sublevel 2 Director				
Manager/ Principal Level				
Sublevel 1 Sr. Manager				
Sublevel 2 Manager				
Designer Level				
Sublevel 1 Lead Designer		Initial career		
Sublevel 2 Sr. Designer				
Sublevel 3 Designer				

FIGURE 5.1. Job framework providing an overview of the job levels and dual careers for the key design roles.

unit, but their executive responsibilities are focused on creative aspects rather than on managerial tasks — even though, similar to design principals, they are also expected to be able to take on some executive managerial tasks.

Figure 5.1 visualizes an example of how a job framework could be built combining the job levels and careers spanning key design roles. When a dual career path is present, a lateral (horizontal) career move is also possible. More specifically, a senior designer can decide to specialize and become a design principal, but then after a while go back into the main career framework and proceed with the role of a design manager. For the expert career path, reaching an executive position is mostly an exception, with the director level usually being the highest one — for example, the creative director role.

BECOMING A CHIEF DESIGN OFFICER

Through the research it became clear that there is substantial variation in terms of job titles for the most senior design leaders who are heading the design function in complex global organizations. The title Chief Design Officer is rapidly becoming prevalent. However, not every organization appoints design leaders who operate at the highest executive level as the CDO. The titles of the most highly ranked executive design leaders encountered in our research are

- Chief Design Officer;
- General Manager, Design;
- (Global) Head of Design.

Within these titles, the "design" designation may be expressed differently. Executive design leaders may be called Chief Experience Officer, Chief Creative Officer, Head of Strategic Design, or Global Head of Digital Design.

Often, the job title architecture is an embedded aspect of HR policies and guidelines. That architecture reflects company precedents, and so may not be easily changed in the short term. For example, in the recent past, it was more common to identify the most senior design leader as the head of design, even if they were part of the most senior executive management team.

With the emergence of the CDO job title, a head of design may request to change their job title — if in line with the scope of their role — to better position the seniority of the role compared to other stakeholders inside and outside the organization. While senior design leaders may question the value of their job title, they still have an important supportive function to facilitate the design leader's activities to effectively embed and scale design within the organization. As observed by Netflix designer Andy Law, "I think one of the most difficult things to do is lead without a title."[6] Thus it is of critical importance that a design leader puts conscious effort into thinking about and potentially discussing the most suitable job title when accepting a new design leadership role.

Considering the rise of the CDO title and the constituent esteem attached to it, it seems the most beneficial job title to strive for today, when seeking to label or relabel the highest-ranked design position in a company. The CDO title also resonates with more common titles such as Chief Marketing Officer or Chief Technology Officer, which should be positioned, in essence, as peer roles.

A change in job title — to Chief Design Officer, or any other appropriate job title — may actually be accompanied by an upward shift in reporting lines to a more senior manager. When reporting lines for a design leader shift upward, this is a strong indication that the executive board recognizes a more strategic value to design.

CONCLUSION

Having a clear and well-thought-out design taxonomy is an essential step in the path towards design excellence and a way to empower the design team. It allows the design function to formalize its position within the company and offer design talent transparent and rewarding career opportunities that are aligned with the rest of the company.

As they develop the taxonomy, executive design leaders may notice certain dualities that will require navigation.

Actual Taxonomy Versus Preferred Taxonomy

The executive design leader should define a relevant taxonomy, oriented either towards the desired future state of excellence or on the current size and scope of the design function. One key decision relates to choosing to be future-oriented, which runs the risk of being too sophisticated, or basing the taxonomy on existing design demand within the company in line with agreed-upon investment.

Creative Career Versus Management Career

Some designers, when advancing their careers, are less excited by pursuing a managerial role and want to keep developing themselves as creative professionals with specialized design expertise. The latter might be difficult in large organizations in which advancing a career generally leads to more managerial responsibilities and alternative paths lead to a lower ceiling for compensation growth and recognition.

Company Alignment Versus Design Distinction

An executive design leader needs to align the design roles and job levels with the practices and standards of HR guidelines and those of the other functions, to ensure that designers have the same career opportunities and benefits enjoyed by other employees. At the same time, some HR guidelines are less suited to the design function, as they do not reflect the uniqueness of the design profession and the way the design function operates (for example, creative skills, imagination, artistic expression, collaborative attitude).

To address such dualities, and, in general, to succeed in developing a design taxonomy, executive design leaders can consider the following guidelines.

- A taxonomy should be balanced in terms of roles and competencies. It is a task of executive design leaders to enable their team to grow in a way such that one role does not eclipse another and designers in different roles can align their interests and priorities without compromising their career opportunities.
- Executive design leaders should offer a dual career path to their designers, in order to provide opportunities for advancement and appropriate recognition to design talent seeking to continue developing their design craft and thought leadership. Alternatively, specialized career paths should be defined with the same degree of accuracy and transparency as more traditional managerial paths.
- HR endorsement is an important requirement for accelerating taxonomy implementation. The taxonomy should be developed in

close collaboration with HR so that it meets and accommodates standard HR policies and guidelines from the beginning, but also to iterate on solutions that will take the unique needs of the design function into account.

- The implementation of the taxonomy needs to be coordinated with the scaling efforts of the design leadership team so that there is sufficient support in terms of actual demand for design and funding.

Creating a design taxonomy is a crucial but complex task, as the executive design leader needs to take a forward-looking approach, generate outcomes in alignment with company standards, and also use a considerable level of detail. However, developing and communicating the taxonomy in a transparent manner is a key milestone, as it will provide clarity on the role of design and offer the design team appropriate motivation and reward for their contribution towards design excellence.

CHAPTER 6

Design Resources

The most enjoyable part of being a design leader is the engagement with, management of, and mentoring of a team capable of growing and, together, elevating impact through design.

AS THE SAYING GOES, a leader is only as good as their team. Effective leaders make sure they have a great team behind them, because it is quite difficult to achieve greatness alone.

This chapter details what design leaders can do to support the growth and thriving of design teams in ways that contribute to organizational success. The activities are clustered into two core areas: effective talent management and the establishment of conditions that enable design to flourish (see Figure 6.1).

Core activities for effective design talent management include

- attract and retain "talented" designers to build design excellence;
- manage and foster design team awareness of their performance objectives and how to reach them, and provide relevant enabling conditions and feedback along the way;
- recognize design team achievements and celebrate professional advancement.

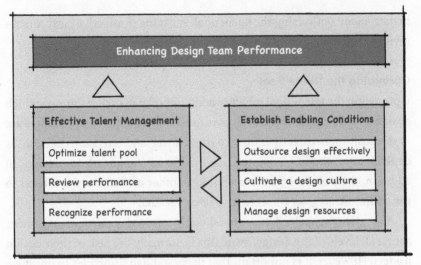

FIGURE 6.1. Activities to enhance design team performance.

Core activities to establish the enabling conditions for great design are

- outsource effectively, to allow the design team to focus on tasks that are central to organizational success;
- cultivate a design culture that energizes and empowers the designers;
- manage the design resources needed for the design team to deliver top performance.

Enhancing design team performance requires design leaders to adhere to both sets of activities. In fact, the activities intertwine — an inspiring design culture helps attract and retain design talent, for example, and providing the design team with the necessary resources helps them reach their objectives. The two sets of activities will be discussed in more detail in the paragraphs that follow.

EFFECTIVE TALENT MANAGEMENT

Effective design talent management is essential to reach design excellence. In this section, we will discuss the following core elements of design talent management: optimizing the talent pool, engaging in effective performance reviews, and recognizing outstanding performance.

Optimizing the Talent Pool

Optimizing the talent pool includes activities related to decisions on which designers to hire and which designers to retain. Whether design leaders are in the position to directly influence these hiring and retention decisions is dependent on the implemented organizational framework for design. In addition, the decision on the preferred number of designers is related to the scaling strategy of the executive design leader.

Executive design leaders are not directly involved in talent management across all levels of the design team; this is normally the task of their design leaders. However, it is important that they establish principles to optimize the talent pool. Some important principles to consider are the following.

Hire competent design leaders. Executive design leaders may not be directly involved in design talent management across all design levels, as noted earlier. However, they should be hands-on involved when hiring design leaders who will become part of the design leadership team and provide support in the overall management of the design team. Attracting and hiring the right design leaders will truly facilitate the job of the executive design leader, as it allows for effective management of responsibilities. The ability to delegate to trusted design leaders will create more time for the executive design leader to engage in strategic activities and work *on* the (design) business, rather than *in* the (design) business.[1]

Members in the design leadership team should support the executive design leader to cascade the design management agenda into the organization and be a custodian for its implementation. When hiring design leaders, design executives indicated that they look for creative professionals who are diverse in terms of background and experiences as they have the ability to empathize with and navigate the wide range of perspectives as found in large, complex organizations. A former vice president of global design at GE Healthcare adopted the following recruitment strategy to build the design team:

This may sound cliché, but I've always tried to hire people who are smarter than me. I don't know everything. . . . I do try to surround myself with incredibly talented people whenever I can, in order to create the sort of ensemble that does drive the power of design. One that garners respect from the company.[2]

Another principle to consider for hiring design leaders is whether they have performed not only design but also business-related roles or have designed for a diverse range of industries. The global design director from a consumer-packaged goods company explicitly looks for "creative directors with a business hat on who know how to operate in an organization like this."

Have affinity with core values. Design leaders furthermore suggested that their new hires must have affinity with the core principles or values of their design function. When there is a potential disconnect, this could negatively influence employee motivation and, in the end, retention. For example, the CDO of a financial services company uses design values to signal the characteristics of the design team to design professionals who are potentially interested in joining the team, but also to question and probe potential candidates on their alignment to the values of the design team during the job interview. Next to having affinity with the design values, it is equally important that new design hires subscribe to overarching company values.

A senior design executive at a multinational in distribution and retailing, for example, aimed to hire design leaders who are "design entrepreneurs at heart" as the company highly values intrapreneurship of its leaders. Indeed, a company's values not only may motivate and help to retain design talent; these values may also attract design talent in the first place. The CDO in the healthcare industry indicated that the organization's values, which include being passionate about improving healthcare, facilitated attracting design talent. To employ designers who have affinity with the values of the design function and the company at large, these values may already be specified in their job description ("You are the type of designer who cares about . . .").[3]

Work together with educational institutions. To attract and recruit new design talent and gain different perspectives, many of the design leaders interviewed work together with (local) colleges, universities, and schools, offering design internships to design students and/or doing research projects together with design students and academic staff. Collaboration with educational institutes also gives opportunities to demonstrate thought leadership of the design team and may support the education of new emerging design talent through guest lectures. As noted by the head of design of a telecommunications company, while their research projects with design colleges normally do not give concrete outcomes for the business (like new products or services which can be introduced to the market), "these projects stimulate me and give me joy; they also create opportunities to find new design talent." Within 3M Design, students can apply for a "Design Internship Experience." These design internships typically span ten to twelve weeks during summertime and take place in 3M's global design center at their headquarters in Maplewood, Minnesota. The design internship program starts with a week-long "Design Base Camp" during which the design interns will be introduced to general topics such as branding and design thinking and have meet-ups and chats with members of the design leadership team. Then the design interns will work on real-life design projects sponsored by the business groups, and will be fully integrated as a member of the project team, while being guided by dedicated 3M designers acting as their supervisors. Supporting these young designers is considered essential to fuel the future pipeline of design talent within 3M. Indeed, design interns often end up being offered an extension of their internship that might result in a full-time position within 3M, depending on where they are in their education.[4]

Hire for diversity. Hiring policy should specifically be aimed at hiring for diversity, to enhance the team's innovativeness and problem-solving competencies, particularly in a global context.[5] Hiring for diversity implies finding a balance in the design team in terms of people demonstrating diversity in thought. This can be achieved by hiring people with diverse experiences, in terms of both work *and* life in general. Having diverse experiences is, in turn, influenced by demographic characteristics such as, for example, education, age, race, gender, or sexual orientation. While it is important to attract designers who subscribe to the broad, overarching values of the design function and the organization at large (see above), this does not mean that new hires need to look at the world in the same manner as the rest of the team. Rather than hiring for "cultural fit," it may be more beneficial to hire for "cultural enrichment."[6] New hires, for example, may not necessarily have to subscribe to the current ways of working in terms of which design tools or methods are used and how. Nor may new designers necessarily have to subscribe to the current (design) strategy. On the contrary, it is through fresh, different perspectives and constructive criticism that the design team can improve and flourish, also in the longer term. Indeed, creating a culture in which people feel free and have a safe space to speak up and challenge assumptions is essential to drive progress, learning, and personal growth across the design team and will in the end have a positive impact on overall team performance. Executive design leaders and their leadership teams have a crucial role to play to lead by example and create a culture that embraces diversity.

Employ effective onboarding of new designers. In terms of new employee engagement, design leaders should develop an effective design onboarding program for new design hires to enhance the new employee experience, while improving the odds of employee retention. At IBM, for example, newly hired designers generally attend a six-week boot camp called "Patterns," taking place at IBM's Austin campus. During this training camp, the new design hires learn how to practice their design craft within the IBM context before they go work in their dedicated business units or functions. The first part of this training is spent on lecture-style presentations about IBM's design tools, systems, and methods, including IBM's Enterprise Design Thinking framework (see more on this design thinking framework further on). In addition, it includes learnings centered on career possibilities within IBM, soft skills, and IBM as a business. The second part of the training camp includes working on an "incubator" team project, provided (sponsored) by an actual IBM team; this is a hands-on project in which the new designers are invited to find a solution to a particular problem, using the newly acquired knowledge, methods, and tools.[7]

Invest in talent development. Talent development of designers is investing in "people equity," helping employees to enhance their individual performance.[8] It is also important from an overarching design function perspective. For example, when the strategy of the design leaders is to scale design not only quantitatively but also qualitatively, design team members may need to be upskilled accordingly. Overall, training and upskilling of the design team may be organized in different ways.

- In-company workshops and training sessions may be organized for design team members to learn about relevant design methods, practices, or tools that are new or substantially updated. For example, training may be provided on how to write effective design briefs together with organizational stakeholders other than designers. Design leaders may also accommodate for dedicated design lectures, or "design summits," where external speakers are invited to present to the design team (and others) on relevant developments, trends, or experiences. For example, 3M Design introduced the so-called "Design Vitamins" program under which experts across a broad spectrum of creative fields or related topics are invited to give presentations to the design team, for example, about strategic design, effective storytelling, inclusive design, creative inspiration, or design futures.
- Next to in-company activities, relevant training and upskilling may also take place offsite, by recognized educational institutions.
- In addition, an effective mentoring system may be set up within which experienced designers are coupled with emerging designers, for example, to become a "buddy" to new recruits or assist those who seek to further develop their skills in a certain design area. As observed by a head of design of an automotive manufacturer, their mentoring system is considered to be "very rewarding for our designers, both for the young and the more experienced ones."

Organizations tend to focus their company training curricula on general business and leadership training programs or very specific technical topics. More specific design-related training is often not covered by these company programs. As a consequence, the design team may have to develop specific design training themselves or in collaboration with external vendors.

Pursue healthy turnover. In terms of retaining designers or letting them go, some of the design leaders interviewed emphasized that a certain amount of turnover of designers is "healthy." Turnover is healthy both from the perspective of the individual designer, who may have more attractive growth opportunities elsewhere, and from the perspective of the design team, which may benefit from the fresh perspectives and experiences new hires can bring. As indicated by a head of design in the aerospace industry, it is "a fine balance" between "keeping good designers," as they are highly sought after in the world and very hard to find in the first place, and "bringing in fresh blood" to advance the design team. Sometimes designers have career ambitions that cannot be fulfilled, in the short or medium term, within the organization. Sometimes the values or objectives of the individual designer versus those of the design function and organization at large may have drifted apart, affecting motivation and commitment. It might also be that the kind of design projects offered are not attractive and challenging anymore for the designer. In both cases, design leaders' enabling of these designers to find another opportunity outside the company is of benefit for both parties. In the end, a design leader is in charge of managing the design talent pool and therefore is responsible to manage this in a way that the quality, diversity, and career growth of individual designers can be supported across the global design team and is of benefit to the overall design function.

Reviewing Design Performance

Performance management is strongly connected with design talent management. When effective, it facilitates designers' understanding of what is expected of them in terms of objectives to reach and helps them grow by receiving feedback on how to further improve their performance and advance their careers.

Performance objectives. To evaluate performance, design leaders normally have ongoing dialogues with each of their subordinates to define and monitor performance goals. During these dialogues, the design leader may stimulate designers to set objectives and agree on expectations that are covering different aspects, including the following:

- *Personal design objectives*, such as further development of personal skills like advancing storytelling abilities through training or gaining leadership experience
- *Functional design objectives*, such as the deployment of design thinking in business innovation teams and engaging in design thought leadership
- *Business design objectives*, such as a focus on design activities that support business priorities in an effective and efficient way and being a cross-functional collaborator.

These three types of objectives are described in Chapter 3, "Design Direction." Which three types of objectives will be emphasized to evaluate individual performance is dependent on the circumstances. For example, a more senior designer in a leadership position may have fewer personal objectives than functional and business design objectives. Furthermore, whether or not designers have solid versus dotted reporting lines into a business group or the design function will generally determine the number of functional versus business design objectives. Overall, the design leader should make sure that the overarching objectives and strategies of the company are "cascaded" and ultimately end up among the relevant objectives on the individual designers' level. This will assist in actually realizing these strategic objectives. In the words of a head of design from a lighting solutions company,

First, we translate the company strategy into a specific design strategy, selecting priorities. Then, to make sure that this strategy is acted upon, we bake its main objectives into the individual KPIs of our designers.

Performance evaluation cycle. In terms of the evaluation cycle for performance reviews, often this is done annually, but more and more companies adopt more "real time" evaluation. The latter approach replaces or complements annual performance reviews with more frequent, informal feedback or feedforward sessions between managers and employees. These more "real time" evaluations help to improve current and future behavior rather than review past behavior. It is an approach in which performance appraisal of management shifts to offering rich feedback during frequent, more informal check-ins to help employees grow and stimulate desired behavior on the job instead of end-of-the-year judgment based on the designer's contributions and rather abstract feedback. This approach not only allows employees to apply feedback more effectively, it also accommodates very dynamic environments in which annual goals may change rapidly and might need to be updated quarterly instead of annually. Furthermore, it accommodates the trend of working in a more agile way, under which projects are broken down into short, time-boxed activities and ongoing debriefing and evaluation sessions.[9]

The "real time" evaluation approach may fully replace annual performance reviews. If so, employees will still set their personal goals, but these are then short term in nature (such as quarterly goals) and will still be aligned to relevant organizational goals (for example, specific outcomes of projects could be linked to overarching organizational goals). The approach can also be complementary, when there is still an end-of-year review, for example to summarize the performance discussions that happened through the year and subsequently focus on career development and rewards. What is important in both approaches, however, is the general principle that leadership is responsible for inspiring, motivating, and guiding designers on the basis of their achievements, ambitions, and possible areas for learning: what should the designer "stop doing," "continue to do," and "start doing?"

Self-evaluation. Executive design leaders are in general involved in performance evaluations of their direct reports, which normally are those within the design leadership team. These performance reviews, whether at the end of the year and/or throughout the year, may be used as a benchmark to evaluate one's own performance as an executive design leader. This implies asking members of the design leadership team questions such as, "What can I, as executive design leader, do (better) to support you professionally and personally?" This upward evaluation approach will give the design leaders in the team the opportunity to give structured feedback about leadership style or management effectiveness. This bottom-up feedback will encourage a learning organization across all levels. Effective application of this bottom-up feedback will, however, depend on the culture and values within the design team and organization at large.

Quantitative and qualitative performance metrics. When evaluating the performance of the design team, a design leader will understand that design is a creative profession in which creative exploration and failure are great ways to learn valuable lessons. Traditional quantitative metrics might not offer a thorough picture to monitor and measure the progress and impact of designers. When reviewing performance of their direct reports, design leaders may want to establish both quantitative *and* qualitative ways of assessing progress and impact. For example, next to measuring projects' outcomes (for example, number of new products supported to be introduced on the market), a design leader may also evaluate the process (for example, the degree to which the designer was involved as a true strategic partner). The performance measures for design should also be aligned with general review practices within the organization as set by HR function. However, human resource practices may offer some flexibility to adapt to a more suitable approach for a creative design function.

Individual versus team performance. When making an assessment and offering feedback, design leaders may need to balance between assessing and optimizing individual performance versus assessing and optimizing team performance. Great outcomes nowadays are often based on cross-functional teamwork. Research suggests that over the last two decades, due to businesses becoming increasingly global and cross-functional, the time spent by managers and employees in collaborative activities has increased by 50 percent or more.[10] Performance evaluations should be adjusted accordingly, rewarding not only individual achievements but also team achievements. One way for a design leader to stimulate designers to excel in terms of both individual and team achievements, and then to recognize this, is to set functional (design) and business (design) objectives, instead of only personal (design) objectives, as we described earlier. Other ways to identify and reward collaboration are, for example, peer recognition programs, or asking feedback on someone's collaborative contributions from a diverse group of colleagues.[11]

Recognizing Outstanding Performance

An important element of design talent management is effective rewarding to inspire the design team to deliver great design work on an ongoing basis.

This will also have a positive influence on employee retention. As an SVP of design from a software and services company observed, "It is important to make sure the team consists of happy designers who want to come to work, want to be challenged, and want to grow so they can give their best design work."

To reward and inspire the design team and retain the most-talented designers, design leaders can use different incentives that can stimulate extrinsic and/or intrinsic motivation. Often the HR function of an organization has defined a package of incentive instruments and guidelines on how to apply these. These instruments are also available to the design function and are great to use as a reward system for the designers. We will discuss some of these instruments in more detail.

Salary-related. To recognize designers for learning, growing, and adding value, there are the traditional financial-related incentives, such as performance-related bonuses and annual salary raise.

Promotion. To motivate designers, having a defined and explicit career framework that provides a taxonomy of design roles and explicates the required competencies for each progressive role is important. By means of such a career framework, people have clarity about growth possibilities within the design function and will know, up front, which competencies to develop to reach the next step. When a designer progresses well in their career and demonstrates being able to handle extended responsibilities they could be promoted to a manager or director role when such a role is vacant in the organization. More on how to structure a design career framework can be found in Chapter 5, "Design Taxonomy."

Lateral role change. To enrich the designers' learning and broadening their experiences and competencies, also over the longer term, another option is to switch design roles laterally, transferring them to another product category, to a different geographic location, or to a new design competency role. This allows the designers to become more "rounded," while it also provides for "healthy rotation," cross-pollination, and fresh perspectives across businesses, functions, or geographic locations.

Inspiration-related. Other, less institutionalized, ways to assist designers on their personal learnings and growth include supporting them in visiting relevant international conferences, exhibitions, or design studios.

Some of the organizations accommodate for employees who wish to act, for a certain period, as a volunteer on a social, not-for-profit project outside their organization. Allowing designers to engage in these activities is very rewarding and contributes to their personal and professional development. In the words of a design director from consumer-packaged goods company,

> For designers, it is important to feed the mind and be inspired by experiencing new trends, developments, and different environments.

Peer recognition. Many of the design leaders interviewed pointed to the importance of creating possibilities for designers to share, on a regular basis, project results with their colleagues. These meetings not only allow for peer recognition, which can be motivational, but also facilitate information sharing and peer feedback. Meetings can take place in a face-to-face manner or via digital platforms. For example, the CDO of a furniture company makes sure designers, working across different businesses, come together at least once a month, using a digital platform, to have a dialogue about their project results. During these meetings, the designers who present their work will have an opportunity "to shine," while for the other designers it is an opportunity "to be inspired by work that they may not have known about." Meetings may be for (parts of) the design team or for a broader group of stakeholders. Indeed, opening up these project-sharing sessions for a broader audience, particularly for stakeholders outside the design team, may facilitate adoption of the ultimate design outcomes, as it may create understanding and appreciation for design.

Related, it may also be an opportunity for members of the design team to share their design projects externally, for example at relevant conferences, during TED Talks, or by doing podcasts. This also supports the careers of individual designers by cultivating exposure and thought leadership.

Creative challenges. Furthermore, opportunities to work on projects that provide for the "right creative challenges" is important to inspire designers: "great designers want great problems to solve," as was shared by the vice president of design of a computer hardware and software company. Indeed, as the design director of a fast-moving consumer goods company observed, "the most important reward is the job" when designers are given great creative challenges to work on and some creative freedom to "push boundaries," which then results in great products commercialized at scale.

Sometimes, however, due to the business context, the portfolio and scope of projects the design team works on may lack sufficient opportunities for designers to truly transform and shape future directions. To rebalance such a portfolio, a VP of design of a healthcare company formulates one or two projects per year that allow designers to explore future design avenues, inviting them to "think big." Such projects are normally funded by means of the budget assigned to the executive design leader rather than the budgets of the business units. These projects are considered of benefit primarily to "bring inspiration" and "retain talented designers," rather than to bring short-term business results. Overall, to attract and retain design talent, design leadership needs to make sure that design projects are creatively challenging and offer an opportunity beyond incremental and obvious expectations. Instead, design projects should, in part, include more transformational, aspirational activities, such as exploring new markets or radically improving customer experiences. For example, the design team from a large telecommunications company was involved in the digital transformation efforts of their company. As shared by the SVP of design,

> We had the opportunity to transform the customer experience for millions of our customers around the world, to affect everyday life in more than twenty countries. That was very motivating for our designers.

Design awards. A mechanism to motivate and create exposure for the design team is recognition through design awards. Design awards tend to recognize excellent design solutions. These design solutions, in turn, tend to be the result of teamwork. Design leaders may thus not want to use design awards as a metric to assess individual performance.

There are many design competitions in existence, and they diverge in terms of reputation, importance, and exposure, with some awards providing for more recognition than others.[12] Acclaimed design awards are, for example, the Red Dot awards, the iF Design awards, and the IDSA awards. Winning design awards is generally considered of value within the design profession since it is an external stamp of approval. However, the value of design awards is sometimes debated. A senior design director from a consumer electronics company, for example, suggested that awards tend to be given to products that are original and distinct but, as a result, may also lack mass appeal:

> If we win a design award, everybody sort of would shake their heads: "Oh no, we haven't won another award, have we?" Because if we win a design award, the product is seen as niche and our business is not to design niche products, it's to design products with mass appeal.

On the other hand, as acknowledged by some design leaders and demonstrated by academic research, winning design awards, particularly acclaimed ones, can actually enhance business performance, as these awards provide for free (media) publicity and can support organizations' marketing efforts. Actual reference of design awards in marketing collateral may, however, be an area of improvement. As suggested by a CDO of a technology-driven company,

> Often the potential value of a design award is not utilized well by the business partners. The effort to submit products in design competitions will not create business value when the business leaders mainly perceive this as a way to drive design thought leadership rather than product excellence that can create additional demand. The value of design awards can only be maximized when designers work more closely together with the business partners to position these awards for commercial and marketing activation.

ESTABLISHING THE CONDITIONS THAT ENABLE GOOD DESIGN

Core enabling conditions that help the design team thrive and which can be proactively influenced by design leaders are

- effective design outsourcing;
- cultivating a design culture;
- managing design resources.

Effective Design Outsourcing

Effective design management is about making sure there is sufficient design talent available to perform design activities in an efficient and effective way while striving for optimal quality. To make this happen, a consistent and well-structured approach to manage design outsourcing is of benefit. The companies interviewed for this research outsourced design in two ways: some relied fully on their in-house talent pool and outsourced design only occasionally; others had a relatively lean in-house design team and outsourced design in a more structural fashion.

The decision to outsource design is not necessarily one that falls uniquely within the remit of the design leadership team. These decisions may need to be taken together with leaders from business units or functions, depending on the design governance structure in place and how design outsourcing is funded. In the end the design leader has the task to maximize the value of the company investments in a balancing act between in-house and outsourced activities.

When (co)deciding on a design outsourcing strategy, design leaders should carefully consider what types of design activities are best to cover by the in-house design team since this has a ripple effect on the competencies that need to be developed internally. For example, at one consumer healthcare company, outside design agencies were used for new product development, while design activities related to branding were predominantly kept in-house to maintain brand consistency and consolidate brand equity. The in-house design team in that case was particularly skilled at branding. Sometimes, the decision to outsource is related to changing demands; outsourcing is then used to work some flexibility into the design talent pool. A head of design from a financial services company explained their strategy regarding in-house designers and the use of external designers:

> Our full-time people are the backbone of what we do, and I'm really trying to help them develop deeper knowledge about how the organization works; and then our design contractors become the "muscle" we can flex to the capacity we need if the demand becomes greater.

Apart from injecting flexibility into the current talent pool, outsourcing also served as a means of spotting new design talent, gaining new perspectives and new knowledge about the latest cutting-edge trends and developments, and accessing design expertise not (yet) available in-house.

The responsibility for design outsourcing *management* — design agency selection, briefing, progress evaluation, and so on — should fall upon the in-house design function. The executive design leader from a furniture manufacturer said that if designers weren't involved in the design subcontracting process, "brand consistency would very quickly disappear." In-house designers can deliver more effective feedback on the (interim) creative work delivered by external design agencies because they know what the work entails (or should entail) and they also speak the language that any designer already knows. For example, the VP of design from a healthcare organization recalled that when the design team took over the responsibility of coordinating the activities of external design agencies, communication was greatly facilitated:

> Designers can talk to other creatives in ways that other functions generally can't. With other functions, you may get feedback like, "I don't like it," for example, or "it doesn't look right." Well . . . that's not useful. "Why don't you like it? Is it the shade, is it the color, is it the shape?" When I first joined, I saw a file named "Version 24finalfinal" — then you know there's a problem.

One of the business units engaging with the CDO of a technology-driven company asked for advice on a rebranding project for one of its divisions. The business unit team had already approached a design agency and received a quotation that came back three times higher than what they originally had budgeted for. The CDO asked to review the design brief of the project to understand whether the agency's approach and estimate were in line with the scope of the project. There was no design brief! The CDO decided to co-create one with the relevant stakeholders, after which it became clear that the external design agency did not have the competencies required for the agreed-upon scope of the project. It emerged that the agency hadn't been selected on the basis of their expertise, in fact, but instead upon the recommendation by somebody on the project team. The design team offered to lead a new agency selection process and used the design brief to invite several specialized agencies to make project proposals and estimates. Given that the design team was managing this, they were able to ask quite detailed questions about each agency's proposed approach, capacity and competencies, related costs, timelines, and deliverables, and to assess the quality of the answers given. After some negotiation by the design team, the project contract was signed at half the cost of the original allocated budget. This specific case helped design to demonstrate to the company that they were in a great position to create substantial business value and increase efficiency. The CDO noted that, in their experience, 20 percent average of the design outsourcing budgets can be saved when design is managing this for the company.

If the design function has no clear mandate from the organization to manage outsourced design activities, design leaders can still influence the process, for example by creating a list of preferred design suppliers or creating design brief templates that will frame external designer collaborations. For more on this, see the section on design tools later in the chapter.

Cultivating a Design Culture

To both energize and empower design talent, the executive design leader is responsible for creating a design culture in which designers are inspired and motivated to excel. What such a design culture precisely entails is pretty open and often not well defined. However, a culture in which designers feel inspired and enabled to thrive seems to be particularly beneficial, also considering the creative nature of the design profession. The following elements may help to create that culture.

A solid design direction. The foundation for an inspiring design culture is to specify the vision, mission, and values or principles guiding the global design team. These components are discussed in detail in Chapter 3, "Design Direction." If well-communicated and embraced, the design direction provides the framework for the design team to operate.

Opportunities for (virtual) interaction. Frequent (virtual) feedback sessions with the design team to evaluate each other's (interim) design outcomes are essential when the goal is to cultivate team spirit, foster active learning about the craft of design, and, hence, instill a coherent sense of design culture. Collective "design critique" meetings are particularly important when designers are spread across the organization or located in different geographic regions, as these designers may feel detached from their peers. Furthermore, regular feedback sessions bolster an essential part of proper design craft execution: reflection. Designers can frame and reframe problems and solutions, and reflect on their design practice, in light of the insights they receive.[13]

Specific meetings may also be organized to recognize successful design achievements, highlight design activities, share best practices, and discuss future directions. These meetings can be made more event-like with the addition of external speakers and team-building activities. Overall, these kinds of meetings are crucial to the ongoing motivation and inspiration of the team and to establish a self-learning and high-performing design organization.

Organizing casual events or doing fun activities together also is part of building up design culture. An SVP of design at a process transformation organization whose annual design team turnover was fairly low (5 percent per year) suggested that "fun" was the reason:

> I'm a huge believer in the word "fun." Fun is undervalued in the business world. We designers don't take ourselves too seriously here. We work hard, we play hard, we get along well.

Of course, what constitutes "fun" is relative. Some examples mentioned in the interviews included regular excursions to museums, visiting a monastery to learn from a priest on mindfulness, and cooking meals for one another.

A sense of empowerment. Even if there is a formal hierarchy in place, as is common, it can be flattened when everybody on the design team feels like their voice is being heard. Empowerment may take many forms; the freedom to work at home, or the flexibility to work outside standard office hours are good examples. As the SVP of design with a relatively high staff retention rate remarked,

We have a really grown-up, fair attitude to how designers can drive their workloads. I assume they are all adults, mature. I don't have to constantly be looking over their shoulders. They know what their deliverable deadlines are, and if they want to work from a beach, or from their home . . . I really don't care, as long as the work gets done. The point is trust — a tremendous amount of trust for one another. Treat people like you want to be treated. It sounds so obvious. All of this sounds like simple common sense. The problem with common sense is, however, is that it's not common practice.

A safe working environment. A healthy design culture implies a safe environment in which designers know that the boss "has their back." In the words of a VP of design at a toy manufacturer,

It is actually really important that people feel safe . . . if they trip over, they've got leadership that's going to be supportive. . . . We're all in this together.

A culture (or climate) characterized by psychological safety is one in which people are comfortable being themselves; they know they can speak freely, without fear of recrimination. According to a landmark teamwork study by Google (known as Project Aristotle), teams work well when there are guidelines that protect psychological safety and promote inclusive behavior. Formalizing the practice of conversational turn-taking and promoting sensitivity to feelings and emotions during team meetings are essential for team members to feel they work in a safe place.[14]

Safety also means that designers can speak up and disagree. Progress tends not to be achieved in environments in which there is a culture of consensus. Design leaders may thus encourage designers to use meetings and discussions as opportunities to speak up, challenge each other, and, when needed, disagree. Innovation is about change and transformation; it often emerges outside people's comfort zones. For example, if a meeting went smoothly, with participants entirely on board with the design proposal, one might question whether the ideas presented were as challenging or disruptive as they could have been. After all, had concepts been stretched beyond preconceived notions, assumptions, and expectations, more discomfort and resistance — which can reveal possible new solutions, and opportunities for greater efficiencies and different forms of value — may have been the result.

Managing Design Resources

For the design team to work effectively and efficiently, design leaders need to make sure it has access to the appropriate resources. Resources can be classified into two groups:

- *Physical*: materials lab, computer hardware and software, and modeling and rapid prototyping (3D printing) equipment; cloud-based applications (Basecamp, Atlassian Confluence, and so on); digital communication tools (Slack); creative collaboration tools (Mural, Miro, and so on)
- *Methodological*: tools to structure design processes, approaches, means, and practices.

Which physical resources are beneficial will depend on business context, the character and scope of the design team, and the types of customer challenges. This paragraph will not attempt to cover all these. The coming sections present and explore some methodological resources that the design function can use to generate and maintain design excellence at scale.

BUILDING A METHODOLOGICAL TOOLKIT

Design leaders are responsible for establishing a toolkit containing the organization's desired process frameworks, tools, and best practices. The toolkit exists to help the design team practice their craft effectively and efficiently. Practices used consistently across the organization facilitate collaboration and integration demonstrating professionalism. Internal business partners should not experience different ways of working by designers depending on, for example, where the designers are located in terms of geographical locations or business units. The VP of global design at a technology company recalled a conversation with the CTO, in the early days of the VP's tenure, on the use of customer journey maps.

> CTO: Every time I come to one of these design reviews, the customer journey map created by your team looks different.
>
> VP Design: Well, that's because they're designers; they are creative and it's how they express themselves. It's all the same information — it's just visually different.
>
> CTO (turning to look at VP): You're making it harder than it should be. Do you really need to be so creative about something as simple as a customer journey map?
>
> VP Design: That's actually a good point.

Following this discussion, the VP of design started the "Better Practices" program. Indeed, there was also agreement within the design team that they did not need "twenty-four" different types of customer journey maps — only three or four. And for every commonly used tool, the VP of design, together with the team, developed standards to guide how they would express themselves.

When developing a methodological toolkit to align designers' ways of working, design leaders should seek to ensure that the tools, methods, and processes used by the design function line up with others used in the organization. Indeed, the toolkit may not necessarily only be available to the design team. It may also be made accessible and shared with other functions or across projects teams in the business. Some tools may even be made available to the general public (such as visual language libraries; more on these further on).

Design leaders must also oversee the methodological toolkit's deployment and adoption; its existence is no guarantee of its use. Design leaders can step up deployment efforts by organizing workshops to train designers in the appropriate use of tools. For example, the design director of a professional services company created a document that explicitly states, "These are the design standards by which we do our work; these are the design values we uphold." According to that leader, many of the design standards and values specified in the document are obvious, but listing them and subsequently organizing workshops with the design team to "discuss what the concepts mean to us, as a team, and also what the concepts mean to each of us as individuals" helped to created alignment and bring them to life within the design team.

To make sure the methodological tools are put to good use, design leaders may include its use in their performance evaluations, albeit in a pragmatic way. For example, an executive design leader reflected that, in a prior role as creative director at a healthcare company, there were three companywide principles (or pillars) upon which every outcome was evaluated. Recognizing the fact that it would be hard to optimize outcomes that embodied all three core principles equally, the design executive adopted this rule when it was time for outcome evaluation: "A project had to shine on at least one element but also respect the other two elements."

Even if the ultimate purpose of the methodological toolkit is to create alignment and consistency in design work, some degree of flexibility is needed when using it, depending on the circumstances. Creating consistency in the use of design tools and approaches and allowing for flexibility in use is, indeed, a dual objective. For the tools to be deployed effectively, perhaps it is best to present them as "guardrails" that delimit parameters while still allowing for flexibility according to circumstance. In fact, that flexibility should be a key criterion when defining the methods, processes, and tools. For example, the CDO at a financial services company explained that when developing a problem-solving approach for the company, flexibility of application was a must:

> The method doesn't tell you what to do in minute detail at every stage. It leaves lots of room for ingenuity and creativity so that design, engineering, and product leaders can figure things out within their context. However, the method does tell you what the primary "verbs and nouns" are that define a certain step.

Some common themes for tools and approaches that might be incorporated into the toolkit can be found in Figure 6.2. The guardrails (top

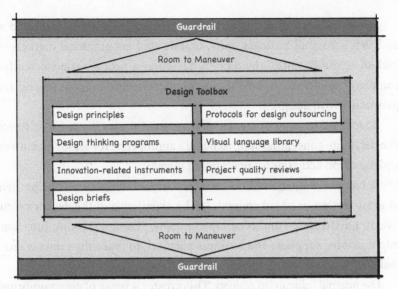

FIGURE 6.2. Methodological toolkit for designers.

and bottom) are placed relatively far apart, allowing for the designers to be somewhat flexible within those boundaries.

Design Principles

Principles are an important item in any design toolbox. They provide strategic guidelines for how to arrive at desired design outcomes. Logitech, the computer peripherals manufacturer, uses design principles that guide designers towards "a single, powerful idea" for designs that have "a soul" and are "effortless, crafted, and magical," resulting in experiences that have "a real sense of purpose, a unique personality, are friction free, are stripped down to the essentials, and are alive and expressive."[15]

Design Thinking Programs

An increasing number of companies invest in design thinking training for nondesign staff within the organization. As indicated by the experience of the design leaders interviewed as part of the research for this book, in-house design thinking programs to train nondesign staff should do the following.

Involve all levels of the organization: "Training should be provided at all levels across all business units, brands, and geographical markets — including the C-suite," the SVP of design at a process transformation company explained, "to show that a company is serious about scaling and partnering with design."

Be tailored in terms of content and duration to suit the target audience: Shorter, more conceptual approaches are appropriate for senior executives, and hands-on activities for operational teams.

Be based on real projects: This keeps participants engaged and helps them to grasp design in (their) context. In the experience of the design executive at a distribution and retailing company, "Design training programs might involve suppliers and business partners, to make the projects more realistic."

Use internal "alumni" as trainers: This creates a sense of community and lends vitality and credibility to acquired design skills. The VP of global design at a technology company explained that one of the actions that made the company's training program more successful was the fact that they "brought in general managers who had been through the course, had applied the knowledge in their business, and could talk about the challenges and benefits of using design principles in their activities — and that was the most impactful thing."

Be owned by the in-house design team: These are the experts who will develop (perhaps with external partners) and deliver the design training program to ensure that the programs are relevant to current organizational activities and aligned with company culture (especially when targeting senior management).

An example of a successful design training program aligned with the criteria above can be found at US technology giant IBM, a best-in-class example of successful implementation at a global scale. From the start of the program in 2013 until early 2018, over 110,000 IBM employees were trained in design thinking.[16] According to a study by Forrester, IBM's approach to design thinking has resulted in concrete positive effects on IBM's performance, including faster and more efficient workflows.[17] Its design thinking program is now part of its service offering to its customers.[18] As noted by Doug Powell, Vice President of Design at IBM, design thinking is not a new idea — IBM has simply adapted its approaches to suit the organization across its various activities.[19] Three principles form the foundation of the IBM approach: user needs are center stage, there is constant iteration, and teams are diverse and empowered. They visualize their approach as an infinite feedback loop that includes the activities of observing (users), reflecting, and making. In order to scale design thinking practices effectively, the IBM approach uses three core practices, or "keys." The first key comprises what they call "hills": statements on interim goals expressed in terms of the intended outcomes for the user (specifying "Who, What, and Wow"), without dictating how to reach those goals. The second practice, called "playbacks," is a series of (online) meetings attended by relevant stakeholders, to discuss work in progress, get feedback, and create alignment. During playback sessions, everybody is on equal footing, and hence free to offer feedback, regardless of company position. The third practice is the inclusion of "sponsor users" on the design team. They are the beneficiaries of what is being developed by the project team, and by having them actively involved, outcomes can be created that truly satisfy their needs and wishes.[20]

Innovation-Related Instruments

An important innovation-related instrument is a blueprint of the overall cross-functional innovation or problem-solving process within the company. Such a blueprint normally includes specific provisions prescribing when designers are involved in the process, what types of activities they will perform, which results are expected from them, and an overview of their accountabilities. When effectively communicated to the other functions, the blueprint becomes an effective educational tool, which is especially beneficial when design as a function is relatively new within the organization. Other well-known instruments to facilitate innovation are, for example, customer journey maps, experience maps, and ideation tools and techniques.

Design Briefs

For every internal and external design project, putting a design brief together up front is very helpful, because it facilitates effective and efficient outcome creation. A good design brief should normally capture the core issue or question to be addressed, specify factual constraints, and serve as a reference to evaluate (interim) outcomes and measure efficiency and effectiveness.[21] The creation of a design brief should fall on the shoulders of the design function, in close collaboration with the other stakeholders involved. Creating alignment early on saves time, as it avoids the need for further iterations and revisions down the track. What is more, the meaningful dialogue with internal and external stakeholders that takes place when creating the design brief can move design from being considered as an aesthetic service to a genuinely respected strategic business partner.[22] Ultimately, however, the design brief is a living document considering the creative nature of the design process; one might even argue that the best design brief is only available once a project is finished.

Protocols for Design Outsourcing

Overviews of preferred external design agencies and/or freelance designers should be created by design leadership and vetted by the people responsible for procurement to guarantee compliance and enhance efficiency. These overviews normally include external designers that the company has already worked with in the past in an effective way. These lists of preferred design suppliers can be used by business units, functions, and the design team when outsourcing design work.

Visual Language Library

To create consistency and efficiency in visual language within the company, design leaders may want to establish visual guidelines for branding or design. These can be published on the company's website and accessible to external vendors. For example, on the website of Atlassian, a B2B software company, visitors can view their visual libraries, which include their brand guidelines and user experience guidelines for colors, icons, illustrations, and typography.[23] Another example is IBM'S open source design system Carbon for digital products and experiences. As its website states, Carbon is IBM's official design system. Its goals are "improving [user interface] consistency and quality, making the design and development process more efficient and focused, establishing a shared vocabulary between designer and developer, and providing clear, discoverable guidance around design and development best practices."[24]

Project Quality Reviews

Processes to structurally evaluate interim project outcomes facilitate quality control. For example, there may be an approach in place in which projects are evaluated for progress at standard intervals (such as ninety-day cycles), when the team is asked to present interim results and feedback is given. Internal digital platforms or channels (Workday, Slack) can be used to share information and interim results and provide feedback.

CONCLUSION

This chapter presented the management practices and tools that will help the design team thrive and attain design excellence. These practices and tools relate to effective design talent management and establishing the conditions that will enable their progress. Some major dualities that a design leader will encounter while managing design activities are as follows.

Being Accommodating Versus Decisive

In terms of effective design talent management, design leaders need to maintain a balance between being empathetic and accommodating and being decisive and directive so things get done. According to one source, successful design leaders are those who "know when to deliver a hug and when to deliver a rebuke."[25] This implies that a design leader needs to understand the art of saying "no," and should make tough decisions if needed to support the greater good of the collective. For example, a resource-intense project initiative that does not contribute to the objectives set may not be enabled by the design leader, regardless of the enthusiasm of the team proposing it. A design team member who consistently underperforms might be encouraged to find employment elsewhere. On the other hand, a good design leader is also accommodating, helping the design team to grow professionally and empowering them so they can operate relatively independently and with pride.

Offering Intrinsic Versus Extrinsic Motivation

To energize and empower design talent, respected design leaders motivate people in various ways. Motivation may be extrinsic in nature — people demonstrate behavior or engage in activities that earn them a reward. Motivation may also be intrinsic — people engage in behavior because it is rewarding in itself. Since both types of motivation drive human behavior, design leaders need to be cognizant of these different types of motivation and try to stimulate both.[26] Extrinsic motivation may be enhanced by, for example, peer recognition, promotion, or pay. Intrinsic motivation may be stimulated by cultivating designers' sense of meaning and purpose.

Safeguarding Consistency Versus Maximizing Creativity

In terms of design management, there is a tension between providing structure and consistency and letting go, empowering the creative process to unfold in a creative fashion. Part of a design leader's role is to create and ensure deployment of design methods, protocols, and tools to safeguard design consistency and facilitate collaboration and alignment with others inside and outside the company. However, the way these methods, protocols, and tools are formulated and deployed must leave room for flexibility and adaptation, according to the circumstances. This is particularly important considering the creative nature of design, leaving designers enough room for flexibility. The ultimate focus should be on optimizing the design outcome and not on optimizing the journey there.

Following are some key takeaways for design leaders regarding effective management of the design team.

- Building a diverse and inclusive design team is essential to attain design excellence. In the recruitment process, the notion of culture fit may need to be replaced with the notion of culture enrichment to instill a more inclusive process. Nevertheless, affinity with the overarching values of the company and the design function is needed to ensure retention of design talent.
- Assessing designers' performance and providing feedback should be done on a continuous basis, rather than solely annually, to help

to instigate current and future behavior rather than review past behavior.

- Motivating the design team requires attention to aspects that stimulate extrinsic and intrinsic motivations. Designers may not only be motivated by traditional drivers such as promotion or financial compensation, they may also respond to intrinsic drivers, such as being able to work on meaningful projects that will impact people's lives for the better.
- Establishing an inspiring design culture in which people feel safe to explore and innovate, make mistakes, learn, disagree, and be creative is hard work but essential to attract, motivate, and retain design talent. An inspiring design culture serves not only designers — it serves the organization as a whole.
- Creating relevant design processes, protocols, and tools is key for design consistency and efficiency, particularly in large, complex organizations. For effective deployment, design leaders need to formulate these in a way that leaves sufficient room for designers to maneuver, accommodating for creativity and changing circumstances.

To conclude, design leaders must engage in activities that provide their design teams with a compelling design direction, an effective structure, and a supportive context. For a design leader, there is nothing more rewarding than having a design team that thrives and is able to influence and impact by design.

PART 3

Elevating to Design Excellence

CHAPTER 7

Design Scaling

The scale of design is determined by its ability to actually create value and influence progress; scaling design across an organization is not a goal in itself.

SCALING REFERS TO THE executive design leader's ongoing management of design offer and demand within the organization with the overarching intent of elevating design to excellence. Scaling design means creating, expanding, and maintaining the demand for strategic and tactical design activities within the organization. At the same time scaling requires adjusting the size and the type of resources of the design function according to changes in demand. To achieve a balance between design supply and demand, executive design leaders can pursue scaling qualitatively and quantitatively. Qualitative scaling means extending the scope of activities in which design delivers business value ranging from the tactical to the strategic. Quantitative scaling refers to optimizing the number and mix of designers everywhere — within business units, at the functional and departmental levels, and at organizational locations worldwide.

The pace of scaling activities and the appropriate combination of qualitative and quantitative scaling should be adapted and nurtured depending on changes in business and market environments and in company strategies. Design leaders can and should be "proactive," by anticipating business and market needs that could impact the size and composition of their team. This chapter will provide guidelines for the proactive approach to scaling. It begins with a description of the similarities, differences, and complementary elements of qualitative and quantitative scaling, followed by some core challenges that design leaders need to consider during their scaling efforts. The focus then shifts to how to generate internal demand for design, a fundamental requirement for scaling to take place — successful design scaling strategies depend on stakeholders' appreciation of design and their subsequent willingness to direct investments towards collaborations with design. Then the chapter provides a three-step approach to fostering appreciation and inspiring partnerships among stakeholders in the organization. The chapter ends by noting certain dualities that scaling presents and some concluding guidelines.

QUALITATIVE AND QUANTITATIVE SCALING
Qualitative Scaling

Qualitative scaling is an effort to develop design competencies at the right sophistication and experience level to deliver business value across a variety of activities of a company. Qualitative scaling supports advancement of the design function from its role as tactical support to one as a strategic source through greater involvement in a progressively broader range of relevant strategic discussions and activities. As the design director of a consumer goods company explained,

> Design was seen as subservient to advertising. It was packaging related, mostly. It did not have a seat at the table. It was not seen as strategic. It was not seen as a brain. It was seen as a pair of hands. . . . And so I felt one of my biggest functional challenges was to rework that definition.

The range of activities that engender qualitative scaling varies depending on the type of business, the ambitions of the design function in terms of scope, and the possibility of stretching certain core design competencies. Given designers' ability to envision future scenarios, in many cases qualitative scaling means joining future casting and scenario-planning activities as a strategic partner. For instance, the VP of design at an automotive company directed scaling efforts towards partnering with other functions responsible for defining the company's vision of the future of the automotive industry. To this end, one of the first acts was to refurbish the interior of an old car with cutting-edge digital technologies to inspire the senior leadership and demonstrate the business impact of demonstrating a future-oriented take on digital technologies.

Designers have a human-centered mindset and ways of working. This means that qualitative scaling efforts might include ensuring that customer insights exert a decisive influence on company strategy. As an example, the head of design at a financial services company determined that efforts at qualitative scaling would be successful when customer insights from design research were a key factor for executive management's selection and prioritization of strategic initiatives.

Given designers' ability to create holistic and engaging consumer experiences, qualitative scaling can also imply increasing design's strategic impact on branding and innovation. For instance, the global design director at a consumer packaged goods company used a combination of storytelling and quantified impact on brand equity to convince the executive board to extend the area of competence of the design function from visual language and packaging to the entire brand experience across all the customer touchpoints.

Since the activities exemplified above affect company strategic decision making, design leaders will be more effective if they have senior or executive positions at both organizational and business levels — when titles such as CDO, VP of Design, or Head of Design have been formally created and recognized as peer roles to the senior leadership and executives of the other organizational functions. Being represented at the executive table sends a clear signal that the company embraces design as a strategic function positioned to influence the direction of the company. As the design director of a healthcare company pointed out,

> You could have hundreds of designers on the ground floor, doing really hard work every day, but unless the top of the organization really embraces design, there's no way to get buy-in from middle management.

The existence of a formal design executive position and involvement in strategic discussions represent important steps in qualitative scaling. To prepare for these roles and tasks, and act on a strategic level with confidence and professional acumen, design leaders and their teams must develop and cultivate the appropriate competencies, methods, and tools. At a computer hardware and software company, designers are formally trained in how to influence and contribute effectively to strategic conversations, and how to establish collaborative relationships with their peers in other functions to work on company strategies together. In addition to this, the design leader must have knowledge about the strategic and operational business planning cycle of the company, so they may effectively anticipate and contribute to decision making and business development together with peers in the organization. Furthermore, investing time and effort in becoming a recognized design thought leader internally and externally can help the design leader gain the recognition, respect, and confidence from colleagues to then be involved to collaborate on the strategic agenda.

Executive design leaders might assess their qualitative scaling progress by monitoring the extent to which design leadership is represented and engaged in the relevant high-level discussions at their organization — when directions are set, decisions made, and priorities defined. Depending on the industry and on the design direction, these discussions can pertain to functions adjacent to design, such as innovation, R&D, marketing, branding, or strategy. Monitoring should be simple and frequent (for example, quarterly). Design leaders should pay attention to whether they are participating in key meetings, to what level they contribute to the agenda and are involved in follow-up activities and workgroups, and also to whether design objectives have been integrated into overarching business objectives.

Quantitative Scaling

Quantitative scaling refers to the adequate amount and range of design competency representation necessary to serve relevant needs at all relevant settings in the company. This means growing the number of in-house designers to an appropriate level to handle the organizational demand for design. While companies might consider some design activities to be non-strategic and prefer to subsequently outsource them, a company aiming to increase the strategic impact of design will reverse the outsourcing practice thoughtfully and hire in-house designers to better utilize design for the company as a value creator. The following advantages will be a direct result of increased in-house design capacity:[1]

- Ownership of the translation of customer insights into value propositions
- Increased brand consistency through orchestration of creative activities
- Safeguarded ownership of design intellectual property
- Accelerated development of design competencies and knowledge
- Greater cost efficiencies
- Rapid adaptability to organizational needs and unexpected circumstances, such as changes in focus areas and project priorities
- Designers' in-depth familiarity with business context and company culture

Quantitative scaling can have different approaches. Some design leaders prefer to have designers or design studios in business-relevant geographic locations close to key markets or core business activities. For instance, the CDO of a furniture manufacturer is focusing geographical scaling efforts on locations where gaining firsthand knowledge of the local culture is important and where having a close contact with local managers is necessary to speed up the development of new offerings. A consumer packaged goods company has recently opened a design studio in Japan, as the country is regarded as a forerunner in technological and lifestyle innovation. An automotive company on the other hand is establishing local design studios based on the location of newly acquired brands or the location of a key production site.

Other design leaders approach quantitative scaling with the goal of having designers in all business units. For instance, the CDO of a technology company scaled design across business units starting from growth areas established by the company. By allocating designers and conducting successful projects in those priority areas, they progressively gained momentum with the different businesses by demonstrating the value of design on the job.

Finally, some design leaders (especially in service and digital industries) formulate their quantitative scaling goals in terms of the ratio of designers to engineers within projects. This approach is frequent in the initial stages of design scaling, to draw the attention to the need for a more balanced composition of innovation teams. For instance, companies using this approach to quantitative scaling include Atlassian, which in five years went from a ratio of one designer to twenty-five engineers to a ratio of one to nine, and IBM, which went from a ratio of one designer to seventy-two engineers to a ratio of one to eight, also in five years.[2]

While opting for hiring in-house designers can be advantageous in different ways, there are still some circumstances in which outsourcing specific tasks to design agencies might be valuable and avoid compromising scaling efforts. For instance, several design leaders interviewed use cutting-edge design agencies to explore emerging design competencies and new design approaches that could be relevant to the strategic goals of the company, but which are not currently available within the design function (for example, design for or with disruptive technologies like artificial intelligence or big data). For companies that need to frequently renew their offering, outsourcing is used to bring a fresh creative perspective or to take care of specialized operational design tasks (such as packaging or graphic design). Outsourcing is also often used by companies with a low level of in-house design competency or lack of critical mass. Using outsourcing might be a lower threshold for design leaders to receive support from business stakeholders who experience the benefits of design, rather than building the commitment to hire designers and unlock investment for an in-house team of designers.

Quantitative and qualitative scaling do not go one to one — a design leader does not necessarily need to increase the number of in-house designers to increase impact or become more valuable. Furthermore, the decision to hire new designers is not only taken on the basis of the design leader's interest in growing their team; it needs to make sense from a business perspective. In the words of the design director at a healthcare company,

We have to be really selective about where and how we seek the big-gest impact — about where our dollars and resources go the furthest to help drive the business in a very profound way.

Finally, the possibility of pursuing quantitative scaling is dependent on budgeting and on the extent to which the organizational framework of the design function allows the design leader to take hiring decisions.

Figure 7.1 shows how design leaders can combine qualitative and quantitative scaling activities depending on the objectives of their design function. When the design function is initiating its scaling process, then design leadership should limit their qualitative and quantitative scaling activities (such as hiring new designers, developing new competencies) and focus on creating demand for design first, for instance by following the steps and tactics of the three-step approach described later in this chapter. Quantitative scaling should prevail when the goal of the design leaders is to grow the operational capacity of the design function to "deliver more of the same, better," for instance because of business growth or to increase designers' presence in multifunctional teams. When the design function aims at specializing as a strategic partner in one specific domain — "doing

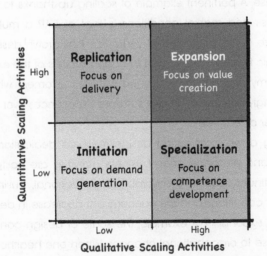

FIGURE 7.1. Scaling objectives and related qualitative and quantitative scaling activities.

new things," such as brand design, digital experience design, envisioning innovation scenarios — then the focus should be on qualitative scaling and on developing the relevant competencies at the appropriate level of sophistication. When the objective is to elevate the role of the design function to the strategic level to maximize value creation, then design leadership should organically combine qualitative and quantitative scaling activities and focus on co-creating value with the company across all of its activities.

CHALLENGES TO THE SCALING PROCESS

Regardless of whether an executive design leader focuses on qualitative or quantitative scaling, scaling design across the organization is challenging, and can be delayed and diverted by a variety of circumstances. As a consequence, scaling can occur in two directions, which might alternate depending on organizational and external circumstances:

- Scaling up, namely increasing design's presence, responsibilities, and (strategic) role when favorable organizational, business, and market conditions determine an increase in demand for design expertise. A pertinent example of scaling up thanks to favorable business and market conditions is that of SAP, a multinational software company. In recent years, SAP has grown design into a strategic function to leverage the opportunities of the experience economy and get more aligned with its customers, who are increasingly prioritizing intuitive software experiences over a greater number of features.[3]

- Scaling down, contracting design resource dedication, involvement, and presence when business activities are postponed or discontinued due to unfavorable organizational, business, and market conditions and the concomitant decrease in demand for design expertise. For example, the scale of design can shrink in response to organizational changes. When one healthcare company reorganized several business units into one, the CDO had to alter the size and scope of the design team to contend with that leaner company configuration and its smaller economies of scale,

streamlined operations, and newly optimized go-to-market strategies. Practically, it meant adjusting the mix of design competencies and reducing the size of the design team so that it could still
be relevant to the new course of the organization.

Many challenges to the directionality of scaling are related to the avail-
ability of a stable and long-term budget commitment towards design.
Companies' realities may change relatively quickly, and therefore budget
commitment to design might be volatile. The business stakeholders that
design leaders engage with generally operate with a short-term perspective, as they manage business performance and might need to change their
priorities (and related investments) every quarter. Design scaling efforts
need to fit this volatile context to be effective. In the words of the CDO of
a home appliances company,

If business is going well, the task of selling in your story is made easier.
If a manager is not available because they are constantly fighting
fires and trying to get costs down and bolster profitability, then you
can't come in and talk about something like what design can do for
the future.

In this case, the design leadership team had to delay their scaling plans
for a year, until the business had more financial bandwidth and was more
engaged and available for dialogue about investing in the design function.

Furthermore, senior management positions change frequently, often
as part of company leadership development programs. This forces design
leaders to continuously educate their peers in the organization about the
value of design and to update their scaling plan every time a new executive
is appointed. This creates tension between the time that the design leader
spends in generating demand for design and the time for actually leading
high-exposure design initiatives that can accelerate design scaling.[4] Another challenge is the competitive labor market for creative professionals
that does not allow for hiring design talent instantly when investment
might be committed and demand is increasing, as a three-to-six-month lead
time is very common for hiring high-profile designers.

A matrixed organizational structure might make design scaling particularly challenging. The design leader will have to navigate and engage with the priorities and interests of other company leaders who represent different businesses, geographies, and functions. As the design director of a packaged consumer goods company explained,

> With this type of structure, functional leaders are hardly more than counselors, as the leaders of the business units dictate everything that happens. . . . They can listen to counsel, and they can get strong direction, but at the end of the day, their job rests on whether or not they are profitable and deliver on their commitments in the business.

A country-specific innovation culture and its potential lack of familiarity with a broader, more strategic perspective on design might also hinder scaling — especially qualitative scaling. The senior design director of a consumer electronics company located in Asia recognized the difficulties that were encountered in trying to convince Asian business leaders to see design as a strategy in the branding domain. The company's focus on "costing down, race to the bottom, and their just-get-it-out-there-as-fast-as-you-can mentality" made it difficult to embrace the long-term perspective and the creative quality that design can bring to brand-related efforts.

While executive design leaders might have a clear view on whether to prioritize qualitative or quantitative scaling, the circumstances above suggest that the underlying core challenge of scaling is to generate and maintain a steady demand for design competencies within the organization. Significant effort should go into identifying which stakeholders to engage with to jump-start the scaling process, which tactics should be used to trigger stakeholders to invest in design more upstream, and how to recognize when a stakeholder is willing to support design scaling. In the coming paragraphs, some advice will be provided on all these aspects, based on the experience of the seasoned design leaders interviewed.

CREATING DEMAND FOR DESIGN: WHERE TO START?

Scaling requires investing time and resources in engaging a variety of stakeholders to generate demand for design. What is the appropriate starting point? There are three main approaches: bottom-up, top-down, and the "sandwich" approach.

Some design leaders start from the more operational level of the organization, reaching out to project leaders and other line managers within business units and functions to generate demand for design. This is known as the bottom-up approach. Once these stakeholders show appreciation for design, the design leader can start conversations about involving designers in their teams (quantitative scaling) and/or collaborating on more strategic projects (qualitative scaling). This approach is effective at companies with limited experience with design and whose focus is on short-term business results. In these circumstances the design leader uses an intrapreneurial approach to scale design and teams up with open-minded, curious managers willing to experiment and partner with design. The CDO of a healthcare company explained that during the first few months in the role, the focus was on finding line managers with innovation-related challenges to solve and who would be open to include members of the design team to help with these challenges. By delivering impactful results and quick wins, design gained widespread support from these managers, who became design ambassadors and progressively helped the CDO gain a more upfront involvement for design within the organization.

The bottom-up approach is a very pragmatic one, as the design leader generally focuses on demonstrating the design process and its strengths and effectiveness through concrete projects on the job. The head of design of a software company started scaling from the bottom up by "demystifying the design process" — developing and sharing engaging playbooks illustrating design activities in inviting, accessible ways that many could imagine themselves participating in, and then running the activities. The goal was to present the design process as an inclusive one, and not only for design professionals. The result was that people from different functions (and levels within the organization) experimented with using the design approach for creating shared outcomes. Similarly, at a healthcare company, the head of strategic design brought design closer to a wider audience within the organization by creating a detailed presentation of the design process through a series of about fifty cases of successful design applications. The variety of cases ensured resonance with a variety of stakeholders at all levels.

Anybody on the design team was encouraged to use the cases to engage with stakeholders from any function or business to create trusted relationships.

The bottom-up approach can be time-consuming, as stakeholders need to be persuaded one by one and throughout all levels of the organization. As a consequence, such an approach is also resource-intense, as it requires engaging in a variety of sometimes unrelated projects to which a number of designers need to be dedicated in order to deliver on high expectations.

The top-down approach, when design leaders are given the mandate to implement their design strategies by the CEO and the executive board, is a more efficient approach to create demand for design. The executive design leader is then involved in the strategic dialogue of the company and is in a better position to create the appropriate conditions that will enable qualitative and quantitative scaling. The head of design of a professional services company felt that the support of the CEO was essential to "navigate organizational politics" and to "model the right, supportive behaviors across the organizations" in order to successfully implement design as a companywide creative platform.

A top-down approach to generate demand for design works best when supported by some form of corporate funding and sponsoring to spearhead the initial stages of scaling, when business leaders still need to embrace its value before structurally committing to design investments. The design director of a consumer packaged goods company described how, when executive management decided to support design's scaling plans, design was funded on the corporate level in the first couple of years, to give the business leaders some financial relief while exploring the impact of design for their business. This gave the design leader the opportunity to demonstrate design value by running actual projects and building proof points, rather than by discussing design impact on certain metrics when there was no base line comparison available yet. Similarly, the VP of design of a computer hardware and software company highlighted the risks of putting the emphasis on the financial value of design too early after the company gave them the mandate of pursuing a design-led transformation within the company:

> I've seen a lot of corporate change programs over my career, and I've seen most of them fail. One of the reasons for a lot of the failures,

I feel, is that they were burdened with success metrics, market facing success metrics, too early. . . . I intentionally obtained a waiver, if you will, that we would not be conditioned by market outcomes, revenue metrics for the first three years.

That VP of design suggested that design leaders could use an internal process metric (rather than a market-facing one) to demonstrate progress and success to important company stakeholders, if necessary. One example is to track the increase in business units' willingness to invest in design, for instance by hiring new designers.

While the CEO's support sends a strong signal about the organization's strategic intent to grow design, that is only a step towards creating a widespread need for design. At a home appliances company, the CDO indicated that earlier attempts to scale design had limited success because prior design leaders had failed to align with the business executives when the CEO gave them the task of harmonizing the brand experience across all touchpoints. As a result, their scaling attempts were perceived as interference with others' domains and did not gain widespread support. To be successful, a top-down approach to scaling needs to be collaborative regardless of context; the design leader must empathize with other functional and business leaders and build on their support, rather than imposing design strategies via CEO mandate.

Given both the advantages and the challenges of the first two approaches, a third one combining the two — the "sandwich" approach — also surfaced during interviews with several design leaders. This approach entails establishing buy-in at the (senior) executive and project management levels concurrently, to be more effective in targeting middle management for their support. This approach is useful when the organizational structure and politics are particularly intricate, and when design interests are very fragmented and not yet well aligned around a shared design direction. The head of design at a financial services company explained that, despite the trust and buy-in from senior management, the scaling strategy was challenged by the middle layers of the organization, where the mindset and management practices were completely different. For instance, to support design scaling, senior management established that a customer experience

TABLE 7.1. Three approaches to initiating the scaling process.

Scaling Approach	Bottom-Up	Top-Down	Sandwich
Key audiences	Project and team managers	CEO and (senior) executives	Middle managers
Focus areas	Ongoing design projects	New strategic initiatives	Design programming
When to apply	- Limited experience with design - Short-term business focus	- Design part of company strategy - Executive endorsement	- Highly complex organization - Fragmented design interests
Advantages	- Pragmatic - Demand driven	- Resource availability - Widespread commitment	- Two ways balanced approach - All levels engagement
Disadvantages	- Time consuming - Resource intense	- Perceived as imposed - Ownership across the organization	- Navigating multilayer politics - Multiple stakeholders
Key actions	- Identify quick wins - Deliver strong design outcomes - Share best cases	- Engage with executive leaders - Ensure funding and sponsorship - Identify strategic initiatives	- Engage at all levels - Identify design ambassadors - Target actions across levels

designer should be involved with any major customer experience project. While this decision represented a great opportunity for the design team, at the same time it encountered resistance. Other employees involved in customer experience projects had reactions such as, "Well, we don't really need designers as we have always been customer centered" or used the customer perspective proposed by the designers in a superficial manner, just as confirmation that design was involved. The design leader realized that senior management support should be combined with targeted actions towards the middle layers. In the words of the head of design, "I think it takes a lot of empathy. It's a lot of conversations. It's a lot of explaining things."

The three approaches and their main characteristics are combined in Table 7.1.

CREATING DESIGN DEMAND: A THREE-STEP APPROACH

Even when the appropriate approach for creating design demand has been selected, gaining the full support of stakeholders for scaling is still

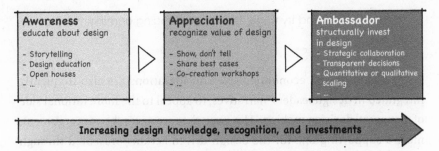

FIGURE 7.2. A three-step process for creating design demand, including tactics.

a challenging task. Design leaders need repeated and prolonged efforts to engage successfully with key stakeholders and legitimize a more strategic role for the design function.[5] An effective way of organizing how to inspire relevant stakeholders to embrace design as a partner is through a three-step approach, in which they first become aware of design and its tools, then appreciate its value, and finally become ambassadors of it throughout the company. Eric developed the three-step approach on the basis of his experience in different design leadership roles. Figure 7.2 illustrates this approach, including a selection of tactics that could be used to support the different steps. As the approach shows, it is only when stakeholders become design ambassadors that they are committed to structurally invest in design and the actual qualitative and quantitative scaling can happen.

Step 1: Awareness: Educate About What Design Is and Can Do

A design leader should start by creating widespread awareness of the value, activities, tools, and methods of design as well as the ambitions of the design function described in the design direction. To create awareness, design leaders should leverage designers' ability to empathize and use their imaginations to communicate visually about design in an effective and inspirational manner. [6] As the head of design of a financial services company recalled,

> We realized that a lot of what we needed to do is be our own internal marketers and branders for design. Every time there was a great success story about design, either one of our projects or something from another company, we would use storytelling to communicate it

to the business and try to get their understanding and their support for our projects.

Factual data and economic value considerations are also frequently integrated in design leaders' narratives, to appeal to the more rational side of managers' decision making.[7] However, they are never the core argument, more a supporting one for the design-driven actions presented through storytelling. For instance, when the VP of global design at a technology company was creating awareness among company's investors on how the design function could potentially help the company make its products more experience-centered, the story first described in human and metaphorical terms how a design partnership would lead to benefits for all customers and stakeholders, and then went into detail about how designers operate and how they can impact the business value of a product portfolio.

Awareness efforts should target as many relevant business and functional colleagues as possible across the organization. To this end, short design thinking workshops might be useful. For instance, the design team of the technology company mentioned above developed a one-hour online design thinking training session for new managers at all levels, to create design awareness as part of the organization's onboarding program. The goal of these training activities was not to turn other professionals into designers, but to develop understanding for designers' way of working. This was intended to make the managers more inclined to engage with design and prepare them to better collaborate with designers. In the words of the design director at a financial services company,

> They'll ask the right questions, they'll ask about the insights, they'll ask about customer perceptions, they'll ask to see the journey maps.

Creating physical spaces where designers can work collaboratively and their results are made visible can help design leaders trigger the attention and curiosity of both internal and external stakeholders. Many design leaders deploy this tactic by setting up iconic working areas for their design teams, which are not only meant to stimulate team creativity and cross-collaboration but also to become conversation items with relevant stakeholders during open-house events.

Step 2: Appreciation: Recognition for the
Value and Contribution of Design

Once stakeholders have sufficient awareness and understanding of design, they can agree to start pilot projects in collaboration with the design function and help them appreciate what design can do through the results of these projects. Here the tactic of "show don't tell" comes into play, when the value of design is not simply pitched in an engaging manner but demonstrated by running actual projects for relevant stakeholders. In the words of the design director at a software development and services company,

> Credibility is established through delivery. And I typically take the stance that "we need to walk our talk," not just talk.

"Show don't tell" can also occur through co-creation activities, in the sense that the demand for design from relevant stakeholders is grown by involving them in design projects. Philips Design uses rapid co-creation workshops with potential internal partners to demonstrate the results that a design approach can offer in a very short time frame and already in the initial phase of the projects.[8] The design executive of a distribution and retailing company also involved business stakeholders in pilot projects to let them experience in real time the value of design. The stakeholders were invited to take the lead in some key project decisions (for example, what to test, what to prototype) to empower them through design and help them develop appreciation of and commitment to design.

Showing successful and impactful cases of design scaling from other companies and benchmarking studies could also help create appreciation for what design can do. The successful design projects run by well-known companies or competitors act as pilot projects showcasing the value of design. For instance, the study that IBM entrusted to Forrester assessing the impact of design thinking practices at scale on IBM performance indicators can be used for this purpose.[9]

The CDO of a financial services company shared with the company CEO the growth trajectories of Fortune 500 companies who had appointed a CDO, to seek support to involve design in more strategic projects:

> I'm like, "We're at the beginning, there are only five companies that I'm aware of in the Fortune 500 or the FTSE 1000 that have a CDO. Apple is on that list. Tesla is not yet a Fortune-indexed company, but it would be included on that list. You've got Johnson & Johnson. You've got 3M. But soon a CDO will be part of every board. Just join me on this journey." That was my argument. It seemed to have worked.

Step 3: Ambassadors: Business Leaders Who Reprioritize Investment in Favor of Design

Once stakeholders have a high awareness of and appreciation for design, they might finally become ambassadors and reprioritize investments or change the way they manage projects to collaborate in an integral way with the design function. At this stage design leaders and stakeholders take decisions together, in a transparent and informed manner. In the words of the senior VP of design at a process transformation company, design ambassadors develop "the ability to spot opportunities to use design as they're sitting in sales meetings or having their quarterly business reviews with their accounts."

Only when this step is reached can scaling actually take place: strategic collaboration with design leaders becomes structural (qualitative scaling) and the budget for hiring designers becomes available (quantitative scaling). For a PC hardware company, that meant that once the VP of global design and the design team had established credibility for their work, they were invited to influence product planning and roadmap creation for different business units (qualitative scaling). In their words, they were able "to see that the work of the design team was utilized by the business, and changing what the R&D or product development teams are working on, and how the marketing teams would sell the product."

Relatedly, the senior design director at a consumer electronics company indicated that initially the company had a limited understanding of design as mostly a creator of aesthetic improvements. However, after one year of using design in customer experience projects, the impact of design on business outcomes was noticeable. This caught the CEO's attention: the CEO wanted to understand the underlying approaches design was taking, and the way to scale this success. Once there was more education about the role of design in combination with the recognized positive outcomes, additional investment enabled the design leader to rapidly scale up the design function from three to thirty designers.

CONCLUSION

Scaling design can be complex and time-consuming, but at the same time is key for executive design leaders to elevate the design function, reach the desired impact, and, ultimately, achieve design excellence. Successful scaling derives from the executive design leader's ability to concurrently generate a steady demand for design and choose the right combination and sequence of qualitative and quantitative efforts to match that demand. In so doing, the executive design leader faces some dualities.

Scaling Up Versus Scaling Down

While the goal of scaling design is to grow its impact within a company, external and internal contingencies (such as economic crises, unfavorable trends, organizational transformations, acquisitions or divestments) might require executive design leaders to reconsider their scaling plans, delay the implementation, and even reduce the size and impact of the design function.

Top-Down Versus Bottom-Up Support

Starting from gaining executive support for growing design as a differentiating partner can give momentum and earn greater budgets to scale design activities upward and outward in the organization. At the same time, executive endorsement for design might be perceived as forced and might not take into immediate account the distinctive mindset and ways of working of the more operational teams, thus resulting in friction. To avoid that and to aim for a more widespread buy-in, design leaders can start scaling from the bottom, working together with operational teams to demonstrate the benefits of design but also accepting the risks of a time- and resource-intensive journey.

Qualitative Versus Quantitative Scaling

Even though executive design leaders must pursue both qualitative and quantitative scaling in order to contribute as a strategic partner, these posit significant trade-offs. When budget is allocated, executive design leaders might invest in rapid quantitative scaling to reach critical mass and gain visibility inside the company, but might find themselves in the situation in which the competencies in the design team are not in line with the objectives, needs, and progress of qualitative scaling. On the other hand, some executive design leaders might obtain a broad strategic mandate from senior management and reach their qualitative scaling goals but lose out on (the budget for) a large and competent enough team to deliver on the strategic activities in which they prefer to be involved.

To address these dualities and engage in scaling successfully, executive design leaders might benefit from the following guidelines:

- The approach to scaling should be flexible; it will need to be continuously adjusted to changing environmental conditions and company priorities, and any subsequent recalibrations of the design direction. Finding a healthy balance between outsourcing and in-house design capacity can help in maintaining this flexibility.
- A "sandwich" approach allows design leaders to capture the advantages of the top-down and the bottom-up approaches in generating demand for design. As this approach gets the design team involved in several projects and several discussions with different managers or executives throughout the company, mastering stakeholder management becomes a key competency of the executive design leader.
- Executive design leaders should strive for design as strategy through an organic approach to scaling. To grow design upstream

and make it more strategic, the executive design leader needs to pursue both qualitative and quantitative scaling. However, the two dimensions should grow gradually and by complementing each other. Quantitative scaling in particular should not be endless, but aligned with the strategy of the design function and its desired scope.

Creating demand for design is a prerequisite for scaling. To achieve their scaling goals executive design leaders should not only plan their qualitative and quantitative efforts but also invest in an adequate set of activities to create and maintain the demand for design. The three-step process for creating demand (from awareness to appreciation to ambassadors) is an easy and customizable tool that combines empathy and a strategic approach to obtain stakeholder engagement.

CHAPTER 8

Design Excellence

The journey to reach design excellence can be intense, but the goal is certainly motivating and rewarding. When the design team is recognized as world class, this comes with responsibility and a need to invest in never-ending efforts to remain at this position.

THE JOURNEY TOWARDS design excellence comes with a long-term commitment from the design team and its leader, as well as from the organization, to engage and invest in a world-class design function. Design excellence is a means to an end: it serves to support the organization on its quest for competitive advantage. Design excellence should be driven by a concern for value and the wider impact it offers to the organization, which the global design director of a retail company summarized in these words:

> Instead of talking about design excellence, I'm talking about value creation for the company — how design can help the company to solve main issues.

To reach design excellence, leaders can use the staged approach visualized in the Leadership for Design Excellence Model (see Figure 1.1). This model presents three distinct phases that are sequential yet also partly overlapping in terms of activities:

Phase 1: Establishing the Design Foundation
Phase 2: Empowering the Design Team
Phase 3: Elevating to Design Excellence

During each of these three phases, the design leader and leadership team need to define and manage the activities of specific building blocks, which include setting the design direction, formulating the organizational framework for the design function, specifying the design taxonomy, managing design resources, and engaging in design scaling. Excellence is the preferred state for a design function in an organization and the result of going through these three phases consistently and successfully. As the head of design at a professional services company explained,

> I would say there is design excellence if design is an integral part of the organization, meaning that design is there, always, when strategic decisions are made.

This chapter will first describe what design excellence actually entails for each of the building blocks discussed in the prior chapters. It will then summarize key insights with respect to the dualities encountered on the journey to design excellence, and how to adjust types of design leadership behavior according to the situation at hand and optimize the appropriate leadership style. The chapter ends with a reflection on emerging areas of impact for design leaders and on how to maintain design excellence over time in the context of an ever-changing environment.

DESIGN EXCELLENCE: THE PREFERRED STATE

Attaining design excellence is exciting and should be celebrated as the result of collaboration, resilience, and fearless design leadership. However, the journey towards design excellence can be challenging and time consuming. Establishing a strong design foundation and building an empowered design team in a large, complex organization can take at least five years. To subsequently elevate to design functional excellence across all its dimensions — when design is fully embedded at scale — can take another five to ten years.

Design functional excellence looks different for every organization. It varies depending on the size of the organization and its complexity, the maturity of the constituent businesses, the types of offerings commercialized, and the number of business activities across geographies. According to the scope of our research, the following key conditions need to be in place to reach design functional excellence:

- The company has the ambition and long-term commitment to grow design as a strategic capability to drive competitive advantage.
- Design is expected to be a global function at scale with contributions across all relevant businesses, functions, and geographies.
- Design strives to be supportive and instrumental to all relevant value areas (innovation, brand, marketing, operations, customer, and strategy).

Design excellence is present when the design team is recognized by industry peers as exemplary and serves as a benchmark and inspiration for other design teams still on their journey towards design excellence. Obviously, recognition of design excellence comes with a widespread acknowledgment within the company that design is an essential strategic capability driving competitive advantage. The following paragraphs describe what the preferred state of design excellence looks like at each stage of the journey.

Design Leadership (Chapter 2)

Design excellence starts with the appointment of a seasoned design leader who is tasked and endorsed to establish, empower, and elevate the design function for the company worldwide. They lead the journey towards design excellence. Because this is a transformational role, the design leader is positioned at the executive level with direct access to and support of the executive board (or one of its senior executive leaders). The executive design leader preferably has taken another organization on this journey before and is a recognized design thought leader. By having the appropriate business acumen to engage successfully with business stakeholders, the design leader is able to build a relevant design organization and culture in which designers can thrive. By making the steps towards design excellence very tangible and attractive through strong storytelling supported by great design results, the design leader is a trusted partner across the organization. The highly creative and collaborative mindset of the design leader enables trusted relationships internally and externally, resulting in exciting opportunities for the design team to demonstrate their value. The design leader is an inspiration to their design team, the organization, and the design world at large, and attracts the best talent to join and contribute to the design excellence journey.

Design Direction (Chapter 3)

To guide the design team into the future, the design leader and their leadership team have formulated a relevant design vision or mission, strategies, and design principles. The design roadmap is clearly defined and incorporates a year-by-year action plan needed to reach the preferred state. This roadmap is updated when needed, but at least once per year during the operations planning cycle of the company. The design principles are embraced and act as an inspiration and guide for the design team about their conduct and the expected quality and direction of their design outcomes. The design direction and all its components are fully aligned with the company's overarching strategy and ambitions. The communication, deployment, and ownership of the design direction are ongoing during the overall journey, and progress is monitored to learn and adapt the design direction when needed. The design direction defined is actually leading the function towards design excellence ("the lighthouse") and at the same time it is flexible and adaptable to respond to shifting contexts and changing dynamics.

Design Organization (Chapter 4)

The design leader and their leadership team have defined an organizational framework for the design function and aligned this with the executive board. This model describes and formalizes the desired ways of working between the design function, the organization, and its main stakeholders, covering engagement related to authority, decision making, and accountability. This design organizational framework has a stipulation guaranteeing sponsorship (funding) by the company for a small center of excellence, and the majority of its budget has been sponsored by the organization and its business units. The management and reporting structure of designers is to the design function (design owns and manages design), and the physical location of the design team(s) is centralized in dedicated design centers or studios. The design leader and their leadership team have entirely built the design function according to the agreed-upon organizational framework for design and are committed (with resilience) not to deviate from this framework and only to make exceptions after reevaluation and in consultation with the executive board.

Design Taxonomy (Chapter 5)

There is a formalized taxonomy of design available, fully aligned with the HR guidelines in the company and with industry standards. This taxonomy describes the scope of design, roles, competencies, and job levels, and will create clarity about what to expect from the design function. The design taxonomy is deployed and respected when building the design function and leads the distribution of design resources into the organization. The design taxonomy delivers a clear job framework with numerous career opportunities for the design team. A dual career ladder is offered to support careers in the creative and the management realms. The cultural behaviors are described on different levels from fundamental to master.

Design Resources (Chapter 6)

The core of a design function is the design team itself, with its designers, since without great designers, there is no great design. Design talent is managed in an effective way, by creating the conditions that enable the talent pool to flourish, managing performance expectations, and creating a safe environment for learning and career growth in which great achievements are recognized and celebrated together. Active mentoring and coaching are established in the design team and internships are embraced as a way to collaborate with emerging design talent who might become part of the team in the future. The team is provided with the appropriate design tools and resources to focus on their design activities and deliver the best design outcomes possible. There is a design culture in which designers are challenged and can learn and grow as individuals and professionals. This design culture embraces diversity as a core principle for building and maintaining a world-class talent base.

Design Scaling (Chapter 7)

The number of design professionals employed in-house has been optimized (quantitative scaling), and these design professionals have the appropriate design competencies (qualitative scaling). As a result, the demand for design across the organization can be accommodated and actively influenced. In addition, the design function has developed to its full potential and effectively balances tactical versus strategic design contributions. Furthermore, in-house design activities are balanced with outsourced design activities, and these outsourced design activities are managed and directed by the in-house design team. The design function is a trusted partner to the organization and its stakeholders.

MANAGING DUALITIES IN DESIGN LEADERSHIP

When shaping and managing the six core building blocks for design excellence (design leadership, design direction, design organization, design taxonomy, design resources, and design scaling), the design leader and their leadership team will encounter dualities or seeming contradictions (think of change versus consolidation). Managing these dualities simultaneously is essential to be effective as a design leader, particularly when operating in large, complex organizations.

The dualities highlighted in the different chapters are summarized in Table 8.1. More dualities will surely arise, but the ones listed in Table 8.1 are those that arose most prominently during the research. An example of a duality encountered when setting a design direction is to formulate a design strategy that challenges the status quo yet also complies with extant organizational strategy. An example of a duality that needs to be dealt with when working on design organization is striving to have the formal authority to make decisions (for example, on design outsourcing) but also garnering the unspoken influence to facilitate implementation of decisions made. See Table 8.1 for the full overview.

TABLE 8.1. Design leadership dualities across the three phases and building blocks.

Phases/Building Blocks	Dualities	
Phase 1: Establishing the Design Foundations		
Design Direction (Chapter 3) Defining the preferred future state of the design function	Challenge	Adhere
	Target the company status quo vs. bolster existing practices.	
	Open strategizing	Closed strategizing
	Open co-creation with the design (leadership) team vs. the design leader working relatively independently.	
	Long-term perspective	Short-term perspective
	Take the long view vs. addressing short-term business realities and changing environmental dynamics.	
Design Organization (Chapter 4) Establishment of the desired way of working	Decentralized funding	Centralized funding
	Design funded across business units vs funded by the organization.	
	Formal authority	Informal influence
	Formal authority; the power to make decisions vs. informal influence, building trust with key stakeholders.	
	Co-location of design	Distribution of design
	All designers co-located at dedicated design centers vs. (physically) distributed across multifunctional project team areas.	
Phase 2: Empowering the Design Team		
Design Taxonomy (Chapter 5) Formalized and HR-aligned description of the design function	Actual taxonomy	Preferred taxonomy
	The taxonomy optimizes the present state of the design function vs. outlines a preferred future state of excellence.	
	Creative career	Management career
	Offer specialized design career trajectories vs. careers with increased managerial responsibilities.	

	Company alignment	Design distinctiveness
	Align design roles and job levels with HR guidelines and other functions vs. creating a unique framework for design.	
Design Resources (Chapter 6) Effective talent management and managing enabling conditions	Being accommodating	Being decisive
	Empathize, enable, empower vs. demonstrating thought leadership, driving progress.	
	Intrinsic motivation	Extrinsic motivation
	Stimulate intrinsic motivation, give a sense of meaning and purpose vs. stimulating extrinsic motivation, offering rewards.	
	Safeguard consistency	Empower creativity
	Provide structure to facilitate consistency and alignment vs. letting creativity unfold towards exceptional outcomes.	
Phase 3: Elevating to Design Excellence		
Design Scaling (Chapter 7) Growing design offer and demand while anticipating future changes	Scaling up	Scaling down
	Expand design function in size and/or remit vs. reducing scope as a response to external and internal contingencies.	
	Top down support	Bottom up support
	Obtain top down, executive board endorsement vs. achieving grassroots buy-in, seeking collaborations to demonstrate the value of design.	
	Qualitative scaling	Quantitative scaling
	Growing design competences to enhance strategic partnership vs. growing the design team in size.	

The dualities listed in Table 8.1 relate specifically to those encountered while amassing the building blocks that lead to design excellence. The overarching, most prominent challenge or duality faced by design leaders operating in a for-profit corporate environment is maintaining a balance between design and business (creativity versus commerce).[1] A design leader needs to find a balance between representing and being an advocate for the design perspective (creativity) and also understanding and being accommodating towards the business perspective (commerce). These perspectives are not necessarily aligned. Business leaders may, for example, prefer incremental advancements that can deliver short-term gains, while design leaders may strive for concepts that are more exciting but might be riskier and take longer to come to fruition.

To manage these dualities in an effective way, design leaders are encouraged to adopt an integrative perspective and avoid a one-sided focus on one particular category over another (such as challenging status quo above adhering to existing practices). Effective design leadership requires understanding and the ability to contend with the complexity of a situation by managing seemingly opposing elements, rather than reducing this complexity by choosing one over the other. Such an integrative perspective is congruent with the philosophical notion of pragmatism, which sees opposing categories as both contradictory and complementary, and also as intertwined.[2]

When translating this to design leadership, it means that seemingly opposing categories should be managed in a way that allows for "and/both" outcomes, rather than "either/or" outcomes.[3] As suggested in the literature, great leaders are those who can reframe strategic challenges from the "tyranny of the or" to the "genius of the and."[4] For example, design scaling can be quantitative or qualitative in nature, focused on an increase either in numbers or in quality. To be effective, however, a design leader may have to accomplish an increase both in number of in-house designers and in their competencies level. Due to resource limitations (time and/or funding), a design leader may, in the short term, have to prioritize one element above the other, but an effective leader makes sure that in the longer term both elements are sufficiently catered for.

DESIGN LEADERSHIP: DYNAMIC BEHAVIOR

To reach design excellence and effectively manage the dualities encountered along the way, leadership behavior is needed that is not fixed, but rather mutable and adaptive according to specific circumstances. It requires a design leadership style that combines and optimizes the following behaviors:

- *Transformative*, yet cognizant of the importance of stabilizing or aligning with what works well. A design leader is supposed to be a change agent who proposes a forward-looking design vision and (radically) new design approaches, concepts, and structures to drive progress. As the journey to design excellence progresses, it is increasingly important to consolidate support and be *affirmative* about the design team and the role of design in the organization at large to leverage the introduced changes.

- *Directive*, to set firm boundaries and execute the direction for the design function. This comes with fearless leadership, the resilience to reach ambitions or objectives and stand tall. However, as the design function matures, more *participative* leadership is needed as it will enable further broadening and deepening of the design function into new areas. A more participative leadership style includes being accommodating to diverse, potentially different perspectives and will include building bridges between design and the other main functions and businesses in the company.

- *Proactive*, to create and act upon opportunities that present themselves for the design function and not ask for permission, as it is better to ask for forgiveness later — when needed. On the other hand, design leaders need to be *responsive* to their environment and to initiatives from colleagues, and play an instrumental role in empowering others. On the journey towards design excellence the ability to be responsive and adaptive is also needed to navigate changing circumstances.

- *Intuitive*, to build on prior experience and navigate a complex environment. In the incubation stages of the design function, it may not be possible to base every decision on facts and figures, and the design leader may have to rely on the power of engaging storytelling and leveraging intuition and experience to drive progress. When the design function has some critical mass, a more *systematic* approach may be needed — using facts, rationality, structured processes, and methods to extend the case for further expansion and pursue growth efficiently.

- *Holistic*, focusing on the main topics and not getting distracted by details. The initiation of the design function needs to be approached with an overarching vision of the desired state and the building blocks to get there. A design leader can be more *specific*, paying attention to the details, when the design function is advancing and focus is needed to drive progress in niche areas of design as part of the ongoing ambition for design excellence.

These characteristics of leadership behavior are visualized in Figure 8.1.

Each of the three phases towards design excellence requires somewhat different types of design leadership behavior, as is visualized in Figure 8.2, resulting in an optimized leadership style. The figure shows that, as the phases progress, the balance in the design leadership behaviors will be expected to shift from the left side (transformative, directive, proactive, intuitive, and holistic) towards the right side (affirmative, participative, responsive, systematic, and specific). Regardless of this shifting emphasis, dualities always need attention. For example, as the journey progresses, more emphasis may need to be put on being systematic, but this does not

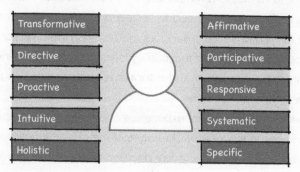

FIGURE 8.1. Core design leadership characteristics.

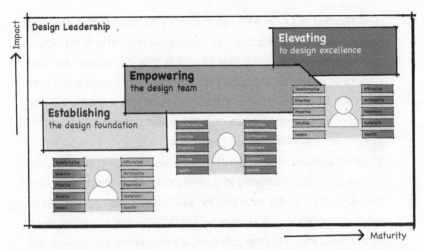

FIGURE 8.2. Leadership characteristics at play during each stage of the pursuit of design excellence.

mean that a design leader relinquishes being intuitive as well. Indeed, as explained above, effective leadership is about resolving challenges with "both/and" outcomes rather than "either/or" outcomes. This is also true of design leadership behavior.

Given the duration of the journey to design excellence and the different characteristics of each of the three phases, the profile of the design leader may differ when appointed to lead different parts of the journey. Some design leaders may thrive when there is an emphasis on the left side of the spectrum and others when the emphasis is more on the right side of the leadership quality spectrum. Figure 8.2, therefore, serves as a good reference when one is seeking to appoint the appropriate design leader to be at the helm of a specific phase of the journey.

DEVELOPMENTS AFFECTING DESIGN LEADERSHIP

From the conversations with a diverse range of (executive) design leaders as part of the research and anticipated trends and realities in the fields of design, business, and society, some emerging areas of opportunity and impact for design leadership came to the surface. These include the following:

- *Emerging technologies*: Artificial intelligence, virtual and augmented reality, data science, and the "Internet of Things" bring new realities and endless opportunities to companies, people, and society. Design leaders and their teams are not only expected to embrace new technologies to enrich their competencies and constantly advance the quality of their design outcomes, but can also play a key role in building future scenarios to evaluate the potential of these technologies and their most suitable applications in terms of stakeholder value generation.[5]

- *Inspiring culture*: Human relationships are changing rapidly due to disrupting developments in society and their consequences on our ways of living (for example, in healthcare, mobility, work). As a result, companies no longer have full control over the creation of brand meanings[6] and the cohesion of their culture. Design leaders have a role in fueling a shared (creative) culture and at the same time in creating brand expressions and inspiring company values that are meaningful and relevant.

- *Advanced collaboration*: New ways of working and collaboration are emerging that are driven by realities of design teams working in multiple global locations and from their private workspaces. For example, virtual tools enable team collaborations 24/7 and give opportunities for flexibility in time, place, and activities to both companies and creative professionals. As collaboration is central to achieving design excellence, design leaders can pave the way in developing new formats for virtual teamwork that optimize the quality and meaningfulness of outcomes. Furthermore, managing company objectives and ambitions that ask for an orchestrated approach, such as customer engagement and brand experience, will have to be leading more than ever with an emphasis on trust, diversity, and inspiration in this changing collaboration paradigm. Given the distinctive characteristics of their leadership style, design leaders have the potential to excel in this role and optimize interactions within and with design.

- *Design for equity*: In the business discourse, the high attention for diversity and inclusion goes beyond hiring practices and asks for a mindset and a work environment that facilitate the expression of and the learning from a diverse community.[7] While design leaders are used to build diverse teams and follow inclusive processes, their next challenge is to become ambassadors of these values and steer organizational practices, processes, and outcomes towards design for diversity, equity, and inclusion.

- *Sustainable innovation*: As the planet is reaching its limits, there is a need for design leaders to be responsible and proactively drive innovation to stretch sustainable goals. When creating new concepts, design leaders have a duty to take the full life cycle into account — from idea to solution to disposal — and unite sustainable quality with the purpose of all people's lives everywhere anytime. Furthermore, as expert collaborators and future-oriented leaders, design leaders are more often initiating sustainability-focused conversations between internal and external stakeholders and influencing the inclusion of sustainability goals in the strategic visions and plans of their companies and related ecosystems.[8]

The possibility of playing a transformational role in these opportunity areas is grounded in the competencies that design leaders already master and that will need to be advanced to these emerging developments. For instance, in light of a broader role in achieving sustainability goals, design leaders will practice their ability to empathize with and represent multiple stakeholders and to be mediators of opportunities with a larger set of counterparts, including communities, policy makers, governments, and academia. Related, design leaders are requested more than ever to be change agents, not only by developing innovative market solutions but also by promoting new ways of working, exploring different values and new approaches within organizations. Their ability to envision future scenarios and to initiate uncommon connections will have to be adapted and extended to the increasing complexities and dynamics of this emerging context.

Figure 8.3 visualizes the mentioned developments and the scope of their impact on design leaders: from affecting design leaders themselves to

FIGURE 8.3. Developments affecting design leadership driving value for society and planet.

changing the ways in which they interact with their environment. Through emerging technologies, design leaders will advance their ability of balancing their expert intuition with more fact-based decision making. Through the resulting strengthened cognition and by cultivating the appropriate mindset, design leaders will engage themselves, their design teams, and business stakeholders at large in more meaningful interactions that will drive value and progress for society and planet.

STRIVING FOR DESIGN EXCELLENCE: A NEVER-ENDING JOURNEY

The world is constantly changing, and companies need to adapt accordingly. Sometimes minor adjustments are needed and sometimes adjustments are major, either temporarily or structurally. In times of great environmental and social upheaval (natural disaster, widespread injustice, pandemic, recession) there might be a need for major adjustments in the ways people live and work together. Designers, with their creativity, imagination, and people-focused and collaborative mindsets, can be protagonists and catalysts to connect all stakeholders and drive progress together in times of change.

Regardless of shifting external and internal circumstances, design leaders should define and strive for their "North Star" — leading their design team to design excellence. The roadmap to that North Star may have to be adjusted, depending on shifting circumstances. Sometimes, for example, timing may require adjustment when progress takes longer than projected. Perhaps the roadmap itself needs to be overhauled in terms of content, due to changing circumstances. For example, due to a change in design sponsoring, design scaling ambitions may have to change. Being adaptive and being able to accommodate these types of changes is an essential part of the job of a design leader.

Indeed, for any leadership role, change is the only constant. In the words of the design executive of a distribution and retailing company,

When I think of design excellence . . . to me there is no finish line. There is only ever-perpetual change; there is no destination, only constant change at an ever-exponential rate. The challenges of always designing and always innovating will be there all the time. By the time you've got to somewhere, your goals as design leader have moved again and you have to switch again.

Because design leaders are seen as change agents, they should be capable of initiating, anticipating, and managing change. There is, however, a substantial difference between initiating change and reacting to change, and design leaders must learn to master being in control and needing to relinquish or reformulate that control when faced with new realities. Every change, be it instigated or imposed, still comes with opportunities, and effective design leaders know how to identify these opportunities and create momentum in the organization to act upon them.

Achieving design excellence may take a design leader many years and require an easily replenished reservoir of resilience and persistence. Indeed, the end state is — or should be — ongoing development and evolution based on new realities, insights, and ambitions that, once fulfilled, continuously advance the design function and the overarching goals of the organization. The journey, when it is going well, is never ending.

Appendix
Research Method
and Approach

The content of this book is predominantly based on research performed in the period between early 2018 and mid-2020. During this period, different research activities sought an answer to one core question: How to engage in design leadership at scale?

The research was motivated by an ever-increasing number of companies recognizing design as a strategic resource that can help them gain and sustain competitive advantage. The research premise, however, was that design is only able to realize its full strategic potential if there is the appropriate design leadership in place and design is an integral part of decision making at the executive level. Unfortunately, there is not much guidance available on how to successfully lead design at the strategic level, particularly in the context of larger, complex organizations. This book provides guidance about effective design leadership in the context of complex and ever-changing environments. To gather a broad academic and practitioner perspective, knowledge was collected through the following research approach.

Throughout the research period, relevant secondary data were examined on design leadership and related topics. These data may have come from professional publications such as blogs, podcasts, or videos posted by design leaders on LinkedIn or elsewhere on social media; industry reports from design or management consultancies; publications by design organizations and institutes; or articles published in newspapers or professional design or business magazines. Articles published in academic design or business journals were also included, as well as relevant books from academic and professional publishers. The most relevant insights from these secondary sources were integrated into this book and full references are provided in the endnotes.

After examining the existing literature, it became more and more apparent that essential knowledge on effective design leadership at scale was insufficient. This was a motivation for Gerda and Giulia to initiate a research project to address this gap. In the first phase of the project, they determined what would be the best research approach to collect relevant information. They decided that, to dissect effective design leadership, there was a need to individually interview senior design leaders about their ways of working, rather than conduct an online survey. While sending out surveys would, perhaps, have resulted in input from more design leaders than the interviews (which are more resource intense), the latter was considered more appropriate; interviews would allow probing for qualitative insights about best practices, tensions, challenges, and solutions that contribute to effective design leadership.

To select the most suitable informants for their research questions, Gerda and Giulia decided to focus on design leaders who operate at a senior level. In addition, the focus was predominantly on design leaders who acted in relatively large organizations across multiple (geographic and industry) markets. This was aligned with an interest in understanding how design leaders would balance often conflicting imperatives in complex organizations that have different business units or divisions across geographies; different functions; and multiple processes, policies, and strategies. The design leaders in this research were not selected in a random fashion, but on the basis of theoretical relevance. Initially, Gerda and Giulia interviewed recognized design leaders whom they already knew from prior research projects and who fulfilled the two basic selection criteria in terms of organizational position and type of organization. These design leaders were asked to suggest names of other relevant design leaders, whom they could interview as well, which created a snowball research approach. In total, fifty-nine senior design leaders from fifty organizations across three regions were interviewed. Of the senior design leaders interviewed, 54 percent acted at executive level (having the title of CDO, Head of Design, (S)VP of Design, or similar) and the remaining 46 percent at a senior design leadership level (having the title of Design Director or similar). When possible or relevant, multiple senior design leaders from the same organization were interviewed. The organizations these design leaders work for are predominantly for-profit organizations that cover a broad range of industries from (fast moving) consumer goods to industrial supplies, finance, consulting, health, IT services, and many more. Their organizations were (at the time) generally larger-sized (a thousand employees or more), operating on a global scale in B2B and/or B2C markets, and had their headquarters in Europe (34 percent), the USA (50 percent), or the Asia Pacific region (16 percent). No leaders from independent design agencies were interviewed, although some of the leaders had worked for design agencies before or for organizations that acquired design agencies and/or enabled their designers to work for external clients.

Each interview lasted from 45 to 120 minutes and was semistructured and open-ended. Most interviews took place via internet-based conversation tools (such as Skype, Zoom, or BlueJeans). Some interviews took place via face-to-face meetings. The questions in the interviews related to (1) the design leaders' backgrounds and their role in the organization; (2) their strategizing activities (design vision, mission, strategy, roadmap); (3) the governance structure of design within the organization, and its pros and cons; (4) practices used to lead and manage the design team on a daily basis; (5) external and internal communications efforts; and (6) practices for successfully scaling design within the organization.

To enhance information sharing during the interviews, Gerda and Giulia assured design leaders up front that the conversations would be kept confidential. They agreed that in any publication or presentation based on their research, all information shared by the design leaders would be anonymized: presented in such a way that neither the design leaders nor their organizations could be identified. Furthermore, at the start of the interviews, each design leader was asked if they agreed to the interview being audio recorded (everybody agreed to this). From these audio recordings, each interview was transcribed and sent back to the design leaders for fact-checking and reviewing. Following university protocols, the original audio recordings and (noncoded) transcripts were only available in digital format, safely stored at approved university storage facilities, and could only be accessed by Gerda and Giulia.

In the second phase of the research, Gerda and Giulia analyzed each transcript. For this analysis, they immersed themselves in the empirical data, reading each of the transcribed interviews carefully, identifying relevant quotes, and clustering these quotes into different themes. Initially, the themes coincided with the six topics of the earlier mentioned interview guidelines, and in additional analysis rounds, those six overarching topics were divided into more fine-grained themes. For example, "design scaling" was split into quantitative and qualitative scaling, and these two subtopics were again subsequently broken down into scaling strategies and scaling tactics for each. When analyzing the data, particular attention was paid to major tensions or challenges as mentioned by the interviewed design leaders and their practices or activities to solve or deal with those tensions or challenges for more effective design leadership in business.

In this second phase of the research, Gerda and Giulia also started to work closely with Eric, who was one of the executive design leaders interviewed by them in the first research phase. On the basis of Eric's reflections on the transcript of his initial interview, Gerda and Giulia supplemented their findings with numerous hours of additional in-depth conversations with him on different (sub)topics, building on the executive design leadership experiences he gained over almost two decades. Most of these conversations were transcribed and subsequently analyzed by Gerda and Giulia. From that analysis, they decided to pivot their initial idea of translating their learnings into an academic article to writing a book instead, together with Eric. After having anonymized all interview data according to the research protocol, Gerda and Giulia discussed the initial findings of their analyses with Eric, asking for his additional reflections. After the data gathering and analysis were completed, the final and third research phase could start; the actual writing of the book together. It was decided that in this book all data from the expert interviews would be anonymized with respect to the names of the design leaders and their companies. All data used from sources in the public domain would mention actual names and companies based on the publication sources mentioned in the endnotes.

In the third phase, the authors combined the learnings from the research and the practitioner experience in this book, and each of them contributed equally in terms of writing efforts. Hence, this book is truly a co-creation effort by all three authors, in which the aim was to write a book that is of direct relevance to (emerging) design leaders that also offers a more reflective, academic take on design leadership — a perspective that reflects the backgrounds and interests of the authors, as a team.

Notes

CHAPTER 1

1. The design leaders and their companies are referred to in an anonymous fashion. When data or quotes are used from sources in the public domain, actual names and companies will be mentioned, and sources specified in the endnotes. We refer to Eric Quint, as coauthor of this book, by his first name.

2. See, e.g., Kamil Michlewski, "Uncovering Design Attitude: Inside the Culture of Designers," *Organization Studies* 29, no. 3 (2008): 373–392; Manto Gotsi, Constantine Andriopoulos, Marianne W. Lewis, and Amy E. Ingram, "Managing Creatives: Paradoxical Approaches to Identity Regulation," *Human Relations* 63, no. 6 (2010): 781–805; Kimberly D. Elsbach, Brooke Brown-Saracino, and Francis J. Flynn, "Collaborating with Creative Peers," *Harvard Business Review* (October 2015): 118–121.

3. Eric Quint, "Q&A," interview by DMI, *Design Management Review* 28, no. 1 (2017): 4–10.

4. Quint, interview.

5. Hans Maria Wingler, *The Bauhaus: Weimar, Dessau, Berlin, Chicago* (Cambridge: MIT Press, 1976).

6. The years as mentioned in Figure 1.2 are approximate and provide the timeline reflecting the role of design in Europe and North America.

7. For an overview of the early stages in the evolution of the role of design, see Helen Perks, Rachel Cooper, and Cassie Jones, "Characterizing the Role of Design in New Product Development: An Empirically Derived Taxonomy," *Journal of Product Innovation Management* 22, no. 2 (2005): 111–127.

8. For research on the role of design in relation to strategy, see, e.g., Brigitte Borja de Mozota, "The Four Powers of Design: A Value Model in Design Management," *Design Management Review* 17, no. 2 (2006): 44–53; Julie H. Hertenstein and Marjorie B. Platt, "Developing a Strategic Design Culture," *Design Management Journal* 8, no. 2 (1997): 10–19.

9. On design making the transition toward a focus on sustainability, see, e.g., Ezio Manzini, "New Design Knowledge," *Design Studies* 3, no. 1 (2009): 4–12; Ezio

Manzini, "Making Things Happen: Social Innovation and Design," *Design Issues* 30, no. 1 (2011): 57–66.

10. On the increasingly central role of sustainability in corporate priority setting, see, e.g., Ram Nidumolu, Coimbatore K. Prahalad, and Madhavan R. Rangaswami, "Why Sustainability Is Now the Key Driver of Innovation," *Harvard Business Review* 87, no. 9 (2009): 56–64; Andreas Georg Scherer, Andreas Rasche, Guido Palazzo, and André Spicer, "Managing for Political Corporate Social Responsibility: New Challenges and Directions for PCSR 2.0," *Journal of Management Studies* 53, no. 3 (2016): 273–298.

11. Giulia Calabretta, Gerda Gemser, and Ingo Karpen, *Strategic Design: Eight Essential Practices Every Strategic Designer Must Master* (Amsterdam: BIS, 2016).

12. On the benefits of design thinking, see, e.g., Jeanne Liedtka, "Why Design Thinking Works," *Harvard Business Review* 96, no. 5 (2018): 72–79. On the difficulties to implement design thinking in large, complex organizations, see, e.g., Lisa Carlgren, Maria Elmquist, and Ingo Rauth, "The Challenges of Using Design Thinking in Industry — Experiences from Five Large Firms," *Creativity and Innovation Management* 25, no. 3 (2016): 344–362.

13. Quint, interview.

14. See, e.g., Christian Homburg, Martin Schwemmle, and Christina Kuehnl, "New Product Design: Concept, Measurement, and Consequences," *Journal of Marketing* 79, no. 3 (2015): 41–56; Ravindra Chitturi, Rajagopal Raghunathan, and Vijay Mahajan, "Delight by Design: The Role of Hedonic Versus Utilitarian Benefits,"*Journal of Marketing* 72, no. 3 (2003): 48–63; Toni-Matti Karjalainen and Dirk Snelders, "Designing Visual Recognition for the Brand," *Journal of Product Innovation Management* 27, no. 1 (2010): 6–22.

15. Liedtka, "Why Design Thinking Works."

16. This was observed by Jeanne Liedtka, one of the most active academic researchers in the field of design thinking. In Jeanne Liedtka, "Perspective: Linking Design Thinking with Innovation Outcomes Through Cognitive Bias Reduction," *Journal of Product Innovation Management* 32, no. 6 (2015): 925–938.

17. In 2018, IBM commissioned Forrester Consulting to carry out a study on the economic impact of applying IBM Enterprise Design Thinking. More on the results can be found in Benjamin Brown, *The Total Economic Impact™ of IBM's Design Thinking Practice* (Cambridge, MA: Forrester Consulting, 2018). The results are summarized in Douglas Powell, "A New Study on Design Thinking Is Great News for Designers," accessed February 21, 2021, https://medium.com/design-ibm/a-new -study-on-design-thinking-is-great-news-for-designers-593f71b40627.

18. See, e.g., Gerda Gemser and Mark A. Leenders, "How Integrating Industrial Design in the Product Development Process Impacts on Company Performance," *Journal of Product Innovation Management* 18, no. 1 (2001): 28–38; Julie H. Hertenstein,

Marjorie B. Platt, and Robert W. Veryzer, "The Impact of Industrial Design Effectiveness on Corporate Financial Performance," *Journal of Product Innovation Management* 22, no. 1 (2005): 3–21; Gerda Gemser, Marina Candi, and Jan van den Ende, "How Design Can Improve Firm Performance," *Design Management Review* 22, no. 2 (2011): 72–77.

19. On the importance of having a design strategy aimed at design innovation, see Gemser and Leenders, "How Integrating Industrial Design in the Product Development Process Impacts on Company Performance."

20. On the importance of design management in general, see Ricardo Chiva and Joaquín Alegre, "Investment in Design and Firm Performance: The Mediating Role of Design Management," *Journal of Product Innovation Management* 26, no. 4 (2009): 424–440. On the importance of integrating designers throughout the whole product innovation process, see Stephen Roper, Pietro Micheli, James H. Love, and Priit Vahter, "The Roles and Effectiveness of Design in New Product Development: A Study of Irish Manufacturers," *Research Policy* 45, no. 1 (2016): 319–329.

21. See, e.g., the studies of the Design Management Institute on the Design Value Index: Jeneanne Rae, "Design Value Index Exemplars Outperform the S&P 500 Index (Again) and a New Crop of Design Leaders Emerge," *Design Management Review* 274 (2016): 4–11. See also, e.g., the study conducted in 2016 by the Danish Design Centre: "Design Delivers: How Design Accelerates Your Business," accessed February 21, 2021, https://danskdesigncenter.dk/en/design-delivers-how-design-accelerates-your-business.

CHAPTER 2

1. As explained in Chapter 1, by *executive design leader* we mean the head of the design function, the person who occupies the most senior role within the organization's hierarchy in terms of design. The term *design leader* is used to refer to the people who lead design efforts for a particular business unit, department, or region of an organization.

2. For a classic article on the difference between leadership and management and that both are needed, see John P. Kotter, "What Leaders Really Do," *Harvard Business Review* (May-June, 1990): 103–111.

3. This chapter focuses on the main tasks of senior-level design leaders. Those who operate on a less senior level may also engage in the design leadership tasks listed, but often on a different scale. For example, rather than engaging in activities at the company level, designers operating at a less senior level may do so on a business-unit level, and rather than operating on global level, may operate on a more regional or country level.

4. GE Healthcare document, "Global Design/ User Experience, 2012," cited in Sarah J. S. Wilner, "Developing Design Thinking: GE Healthcare's Menlo Innovation

Model," in *Design Thinking: New Product Development Essentials from the PDMA*, ed. Michael G. Luchs, Scott Swan, and Abbie Griffin (Hoboken, NJ: John Wiley & Sons, 2015): 157–172.

5. On the need for designers to pay much time on educating and persuading organizational stakeholders on designerly ways of working to, ultimately, create a design-driven organization, see also Tua Björklund, Hanna Maula, Sarah A. Soule, and Jesse Maula, "Integrating Design into Organizations: The Coevolution of Design Capabilities," *California Management Review* 62, no. 2 (2020): 100–124.

6. Sean Blanda, "The Subtle Art of Being a Designer at a Massive Company," *99u* (blog), March 16, 2013, https://99u.adobe.com/articles/60997/how-to-be-a-designer-at-a-large-company-3m.

7. For example, Bernard Jaworski, who fulfilled both academic and practitioner roles in the field of (marketing) management, suggested that the role of the chief marketing officer is to "own the voice of the market, including the voice of customer segments." See Bernard J. Jaworski, "On Managerial Relevance," *Journal of Marketing* 75, no. 4 (2011): 219.

8. Youngjin Yoo and Kyungmook Kim, "How Samsung Became a Design Powerhouse," *Harvard Business Review* 93, no. 9 (2015): 75.

9. See Rama Gheerawo, "Creative Leadership: Transforming Individuals and Organizations," *Design Management Review* 30, no. 2 (2019): 4–9.

10. See, e.g., Eric's keynote talk: "Collaborative Creativity: Applied Design Thinking," provided in April 2018 during the Design Thinking Conference USA Summit (Austin, Texas). On being a "stretch agent," see, e.g., Eric Quint, "Q&A," interview by DMI, *Design Management Review* 28, no. 1 (2017): 4–10.

11. On the notion of designers stretching conceptualizations of feasibility within an organization, see also, e.g., Gerda Gemser, Blair Kuys, and Opher Yom-Tov, "Designing for Feasibility," in *Strategic Design: Eight Essential Practices Every Strategic Designer Must Master*, ed. Giulia Calabretta, Gerda Gemser, and Ingo Karpen (Amsterdam: BIS, 2016): 142–167.

12. The value of the 3M Company brand grew 30 percent from 2015 (when the new brand platform "Science Applied to Life" was introduced) to 2020. See Interbrand, "Best Global Brands 2015," accessed February 21, 2021, https://interbrand.com/wp-content/uploads/2016/02/Best-Global-Brands-2015-report.pdf; Interbrand, "Best Global Brands 2020," accessed February 21, 2021, https://learn.interbrand.com/hubfs/INTERBRAND/Interbrand_Best_Global_Brands%202020.pdf.

13. For an interesting blog on entrepreneurs and the use of intuition, see, e.g., Caroline Castrillon, "3 Ways Entrepreneurs Can Tap into Their Intuition to Get That Extra Edge," *Forbes,* May 29, 2019, https://www.forbes.com/sites/carolinecastrillon/2019/05/29/3-ways-entrepreneurs-can-tap-into-their-intuition-to-get-that-extra-edge/#1d659a6b58bd. For academic research on how designers use intuition and

rationality to make effective strategic decisions, see Giulia Calabretta, Gerda Gemser, and Nachoem M. Wijnberg, "The Interplay Between Intuition and Rationality in Strategic Decision Making: A Paradox Perspective," *Organization Studies* 38, nos. 3–4 (2017): 365–401. For a more general overview about academic research on entrepreneurship and intuition, see, e.g., Leonie Baldacchino, Deniz Ucbasaran, Laure Cabantous, and Andy Lockett, "Entrepreneurship Research on Intuition: A Critical Analysis and Research Agenda," *International Journal of Management Reviews* 17, no. 2 (2015): 212–231.

14. The notion of "enlightened empathy" was used by Joe Gebbia, cofounder of Airbnb to describe the need for a designer to "see the world through the eyes of the person you're designing for" but also to make sure that, as a designer, you do not "design by committee" but subsequently "combine what you learned with your own point of view and your own creativity and your own imagination as a designer." See Leigh Gallagher, "Airbnb Cofounder Joe Gebbia on How 'Dog-Fooding' Leads to Great Design," *Fortune*, December 22, 2017, https://fortune.com/2017/12/22/airbnb -joe-gebbia/.

CHAPTER 3

1. James Collins and Jerry I. Porras, "Building Your Company's Vision," *Harvard Business Review* 74, no. 5 (1996): 65–77.

2. Ramon Casadesus-Masanell, "Strategy Reading: Setting Aspirations — Mission, Vision, and Values," *Harvard Business Publishing* (March 2014): 1–30.

3. "3M Design Mission," 3M Design, accessed July 15, 2020, 3m.com/3M/en_US/ design-us/.

4. "Design Guidelines", Salesforce, last updated February 19, 2021, https://www .lightningdesignsystem.com/guidelines/overview/.

5. Collins and Porras, "Building Your Company's Vision."

6. "Philips Design," Koninklijke Philips N.V., accessed July 15 2020, https://www .philips.com/a-w/about/philips-design.html.

7. Simon Sinek, *Start with Why: How Great Leaders Inspire Everyone to Take Action* (New York: Penguin, 2009).

8. "Our Mission," SAP AppHaus, accessed July 15, 2020, https://experience.sap .com/designservices/.

9. For more information on designers' abilities of envisioning and synthetizing information, see Giulia Calabretta, Gerda Gemser, and Ingo Karpen, *Strategic Design: Eight Essential Practices Every Strategic Designer Must Master* (Amsterdam: BIS, 2016).

10. For more information on why and how to adopt a more agile approach to strategic planning, see Alessandro Di Fiore, "Planning Doesn't Have to Be the Enemy of Agile," *Harvard Business Review* (blog), September 13, 2018, https://hbr.org/ 2018/09/planning-doesnt-have-to-be-the-enemy-of-agile.

11. For more information about adopting an open and inclusive approach to strategy, see Henry Adobor, "Opening Up Strategy Formulation: Benefits, Risks, and Some Suggestions," *Business Horizons* 62, no. 3 (2019): 383–393.

12. To learn more about why and how to separate the strategizing process into two distinct work streams, see Herman Spruit and James Dixon, "How to Breathe New Life into Strategy," Bain & Company, July 9, 2020, https://www.bain.com/insights/how-to-breathe-new-life-into-strategy?fbclid =IwAR1aDFzaRhgdqucgyy7Y4F4R20WUTidOGJJwtUWjQj1lXHYh9ZlTc4JcKBw.

13. "Philips — Design Manifesto," produced by PlusOne in partnership with Philips Design, 2015, https://vimeo.com/139447650.

14. For practitioner reports on the link between design activities and performance metrics, see Leah Buley, "The New Design Frontier," *Invision*, accessed July 20, 2020, https://www.invisionapp.com/design-better/design-maturity-model/; Benedict Sheppard, Hugo Sarrazin, Garen Kouyoumjian, and Fabricio Dore, "The Business Value of Design," McKinsey & Company, accessed July 20, 2020, https://www.mckinsey.com/business-functions/mckinsey-design/our-insights/ the-business-value-of-design; Benjamin Brown, *The Total Economic Impact™ of IBM's Design Thinking Practice*, (Cambridge, MA: Forrester Consulting, 2018), https://www.ibm.com/design/thinking/static/Enterprise-Design-Thinking-Report -8ab1e9e1622899654844a5fe1d760ed5.pdf; Jeneanne Rae, "Design Value Index Exemplars Outperform the S&P 500 Index (Again) and a New Crop of Design Leaders Emerge," *Design Management Review* 274 (2016): 4–11.

For academic research on the topic, see Gerda Gemser and Mark A. Leenders, "How Integrating Industrial Design in the Product Development Process Impacts on Company Performance," *Journal of Product Innovation Management* 18, no. 1 (2001): 28–38; Julie H. Hertenstein, Marjorie B. Platt, and Robert W. Veryzer, "The Impact of Industrial Design Effectiveness on Corporate Financial Performance," *Journal of Product Innovation Management* 22, no. 1 (2005): 3–21; James Moultrie and Finbarr Livesey, "Measuring Design Investment in Firms: Conceptual Foundations and Exploratory UK Survey," *Research Policy* 43, no. 3 (2014): 570–587.

15. The Net Promoter Score is a loyalty metric developed by Bain & Co that shows the percentage of customers who would recommend a brand or product to others — friends, family, or colleagues). More on this can be found here: "Net Pomoter System℠," Bain & Company, accessed May 29, 2020, https://www.bain .com/consulting-services/customer-strategy-and-marketing/customer-loyalty/.

CHAPTER 4

1. The term *business unit* is not consistently used by companies that use a matrix structure. In the context of this book, we use it to indicate an entity within an

organization that has dedicated business leadership to manage resources, investments, and P&L, and works to commercialize specific market offerings.

2. Carole Bilson and Iain Aitchison, "Tips for Building a Successful Design Organization," *Design Management Review* 27, no. 2 (2016): 50–53.

3. For more on this, see Cliona O'Sullivan, "Dialling Up the Joy, Turning Down the Pain: Design Ops at Spotify," *Spotify.Design* (blog), October 2019, https://spotify .design/article/dialling-up-the-joy-turning-down-the-pain-design-ops-at-spotify.

4. For more information on how the Design Ops team at Spotify approaches design tool creation, see Cliona O'Sullivan and Barton Smith, "How Spotify Organises Work in Figma to Improve Collaboration," *Spotify.Design* (blog), April 2020, https://spotify.design/article/how-spotify-organises-work-in-figma-to-improve -collaboration. For more information on how Spotify designers created Encore, a design system that uses a family of design languages, see Gerrit Kaiser, Marina Posniak, and Shaun Bent, "Reimagining Design Systems at Spotify," *Spotify.Design* (blog), September 2020, https://spotify.design/article/reimagining-design-systems -at-spotify.

5. For further reading, see Thomas Sy and Laura Sue D'Annunzio, "Challenges and Strategies of Matrix Organizations," *Human Resource Planning* 28, no. 1 (2005): 39–48. See also Jay R. Galbraith, *Designing Matrix Organizations That Actually Work: How IBM, Procter & Gamble and Others Design for Success* (Hoboken, NJ: John Wiley & Sons, 2008).

6. An example is the Spotify governance framework referred to earlier, characterized by significant decentralization and autonomy, centered around units labeled squads, chapters, tribes, and guilds. Within the Spotify framework, roles, functions, and responsibilities are divided in nontraditional ways that diverge from traditional matrix-structured organizations. The framework aims to speed up product development, a recommended approach for fast-moving industries. Some, however, have criticized the effectiveness of the framework and organizations allowing themselves to be inspired by it, such as the Netherland's ING Bank, which adjusted the framework somewhat to make it work better for them. For more information on Spotify's innovative organizational framework, and the revised framework used by ING, see Ard-Pieter de Man, Pieter Koene, and Martijn Ars, *How to Survive the Organizational Revolution: A Guide to Agile Contemporary Operating Frameworks, Platforms and Ecosystems*, (Amsterdam: BIS, 2019). Another example of a company using an alternative matrix structure is Airbnb, the home rental platform. Airbnb designers are responsible for the hosts' and guests' end-to-end customer journeys. They are co-located in multifunctional teams responsible for different key milestones on the customer journeys. By implementing the new structure, Airbnb wanted to prevent inconsistent and underoptimized customer experiences that can emerge inside

largely siloed organizations. For more information on constellating a framework around customer journeys, see Bharat Poddar, Yogesh Mishra, and Anandapadmanabhan Ramabhadran, "Transform Customer Journeys at Scale — and Transform Your Business," Boston Consulting Group, November 8, 2019, https://www.bcg.com/publications/2019/transform-customer-journeys-scale-transform-business.

7. David J. Schwartz, *The Magic of Thinking Big* (New York: Simon & Schuster, 1959).

8. These design-sponsoring approaches apply to design resourcing in relatively large, matrix-structured organizations. For further information about organizational models for design teams in smaller organizations, see Peter Merholz and Kristin Skinner, *Org Design for Design Orgs: Building and Managing In-House Design Teams* (Sebastopol, CA: O'Reilly Media, 2016). Please note that the approaches for design resourcing as discussed in this chapter are the ones most common in our research. However, the list is not exhaustive. For example, an approach we do not discuss further is one in which other departments such as marketing or R&D are sponsoring design.

9. O'Sullivan, "Dialling Up the Joy, Turning Down the Pain."

10. For more information on dual reporting lines and performance evaluation within matrix organizations, see, e.g., Steven H. Appelbaum, David Nadeau, and Michael Cyr, "Performance Evaluation in a Matrix Organization: A Case Study (Part One)," *Industrial and Commercial Training* 40, no. 5 (2008): 236–241.

11. In this section on reporting lines, we focus on designers reporting into a business unit and/or reporting into the design function. Another option is designers reporting into another function, such as marketing or R&D. Similar to reporting into a business unit, whether or not this type of reporting line is in place tends to correlate with how design is sponsored from a financial perspective.

12. Thomas Sy and his colleagues describe some key challenges related to matrix-based organizational structures that all relate to employee performance. Sy and D'Annunzio, "Challenges and Strategies of Matrix Organizations."

13. For more practical tips on introducing dotted-line reporting and managing dual reporting structures as a leader, see Ian Munro, "If You Want to Make Dotted Line Reporting Work, You Need to Do 3 Things," *Legitimate Leadership* (blog), June 14, 2018, https://www.legitimateleadership.com/2018/06/14/if-you-want-to-make-dotted-line-reporting-work-you-need-to-do-3-things/.

14. The executive board is the highest-ranking organizational body. It oversees the organization's operations, strategic planning, and decision making. It is chaired by the CEO and staffed by that person's direct reports (typically the senior C-suite). It is sometimes called the executive committee.

15. For similar overviews of the pros and cons of centralized design versus decentralized or hybrid models, see, e.g., Merholz and Skinner, "*Org Design for Design*

Orgs"; and Aarron Walter and Eli Woolery, *Design Leadership Handbook* (New York: Invision, 2020), https://www.designbetter.co/design-leadership-handbook. Please note that, as with design sponsoring and reporting lines, we focus on discussing the approaches most common in our research. The approaches we discuss are thus not exhaustive; an alterantive approach is, for example, designers sitting together with another function, such as marketing or R&D.

16. Atlassian's multidisciplinary team configurations vary depending on their missions, and so do not always include engineers, project managers, and designers. Visit the Atlassian website to further explore the latest practices used to facilitate teamwork within Atlassian: https://www.atlassian.com/, accessed February 23, 2020.

17. For more information, see de Man, Koene, and Ars, *How to Survive the Organizational Revolution*, in particular Chapter 3, on the Spotify model.

18. See Nicole Burrow, "Making the Band: Building Exceptional Design Teams at Spotify," *Spotify.Design* (blog), January 2020, https://spotify.design/article/making-the-band-building-exceptional-design-teams-at-spotify.

19. Mike Davidson, quoted in Walter and Woolery, *Design Leadership Handbook*, 40–41.

CHAPTER 5

1. The Hay system is a point-based method for mapping and evaluating job roles within the organizational structure. For more information and a critical perspective on its advantages and limitations, see Muhammad Ali EL-Hajji, "The Hay System of Job Evaluation: A Critical Analysis," *Journal of Human Resources* 3, no. 1 (2015): 1–22.

2. For more on what constitutes a competency and on a competency-based approach to managing a team, see Fotis Draganidis and Gregoris Mentzas, "Competency Based Management: A Review of Systems and Approaches," *Information Management & Computer Security* 14, no. 1 (2006): 51–64.

3. For an example of how different types of competencies combine in a design role, see Hyo-Jin Kang, Kyung-won Chung, and Young Nam, "A Competence Model for Design Managers: A Case Study of Middle Managers in Korea," *International Journal of Design* 9, no. 2 (2015).

4. For more examples, see Peter Merholz and Kristin Skinner, *Org Design for Design Orgs: Building and Managing In-House Design Teams,* (Sebastopol, CA: O'Reilly Media, 2016).

5. Darryl K. Taft, "IBM Launches Distinguished Designer Program," *eWeek* (blog), April 25, 2016, https://www.eweek.com/development/ibm-launches-distinguished-designer-program.

6. Aarron Walter and Eli Woolery, *Design Leadership Handbook,* (New York: Invision, 2020), https://www.designbetter.co/design-leadership-handbook.

CHAPTER 6

1. This saying was discussed by Richard Banfield, among others, in his book *Design Leadership* (Sebastopol, CA: O'Reilly Media, 2016), 74.

2. Bob Schwartz, "Q&A," interview by DMI, *Design Management Review* 31, no. 2 (2020): 9.

3. For other, very concrete tips on how to hire the appropriate people for effective design teams, see, e.g., Aarron Walter and Eli Woolery, *Design Leadership Handbook* (New York: Invision, 2020), https://www.designbetter.co/design-leadership-handbook. See also Chapter 6 in Peter Merholz and Kristin Skinner, *Org Design for Design Orgs: Building and Managing In-house Design Teams,* (Sebastopol, CA: O'Reilly Media, 2016).

4. For more information on the design intern program of 3M, visit 3M Careers, accessed June 15, 2020, https://www.3m.com/3M/en_US/careers-us/students/design-internship-program/; "3M Internships Adapt to the Virtual Work World," 3M News Center, July 22, 2020, https://news.3m.com/English/3m-stories/3m-details/2020/3M-Internships-Adapt-to-the-Virtual-Work-World/default.aspx.

5. On the positive influence of diversity on team performance, see Katherine K. Phillips, "How Diversity Makes Us Smarter," *Scientific American*, October 1, 2014, https://www.scientificamerican.com/article/how-diversity-makes-us-smarter/.

6. For an interesting article on companies going from "cultural fit" to "cultural add" as a foundation in the recruitment process, see Lars Schmidt, " The End of Culture Fit," *Forbes*, March 21, 2017, https://www.forbes.com/sites/larsschmidt/2017/03/21/the-end-of-culture-fit/#1efffe76638a.

7. The information on IBM's onboarding program is based on the following blog articles: Lauren Swanson, "How IBM Helps Designers Build Skills and Grow Their Careers," *Medium* (blog), October 28, 2019, https://medium.com/design-ibm/how-ibm-helps-designers-build-skills-and-grow-their-careers-a3917bbebca4; Eric Chung, "I Survived Patterns: IBM's Design Education Program," *Medium* (blog), September 18, 2019, https://medium.com/design-ibm/i-survived-patterns-ibm-design-3fd9a141db7b.

8. On people equity and how to increase it, see, e.g., William A. Schiemann, "People Equity: A New Paradigm for Measuring and Managing Human Capital," *People and Strategy* 29, no. 1 (2006): 34–44.

9. The provided discussion on real-time performance evaluation is based on Peter Cappelli and Anna Tavis, "The Performance Management Revolution," *Harvard Business Review* (October 2016): 58–67.

10. Rob Cross, Reb Rebele, and Adam Grant, "Collaborative Overload," *Harvard Business Review* (January-February, 2016): 74–79.

11. Cross, Rebele, and Grant, "Collaborative Overload."

12. For an explanation of different types of design awards and why they may diverge in impact, see Gerda Gemser and Nachoem M. Wijnberg, "The Economic Significance of Industrial Design Awards: A Conceptual Framework," *Design Management Journal-Academic Review* 2, no. 1, (2002): 61–71. For empirical evidence demonstrating that some awards are more important than others, see Gerda Gemser, Mark A.A.M. Leenders, and Nachoem M. Wijnberg, "Why Some Awards Are More Effective Signals of Quality than Others: A Study of Movie Awards," *Journal of Management* 34n, no. 1 (2008): 25–54. On design awards specifically and their impact, see, e.g., Whan Oh Sung, Ki-Young Nam, and Kyung-won Chung, " Strategic Use of International Product Design Award Schemes," *Design Management Journal* 5, no. 1 (2010): 72–86; Yusen Xia, Vinod Singhal, and Peter G. Zhang, "Product Design Awards and the Market Value of the Firm," *Production and Operations Management* 25, no. 6 (2016): 1038–1055.

13. For a philosophical discussion on design as reflective practice, see Donald Schon, *The Reflective Practitioner: How Professionals Think in Action* (New York, Basic Books: 1983). For a more concrete discussion of various forms of feedback opportunities, such as design reviews, design stand-ups, retrospectives, and post mortems, see Walter and Woolery, *Design Leadership Handbook.*

14. For more on Google's landmark project Aristotle, and to learn how to create psychologically safe environments for teams, see Charles Duhigg, "What Google Learned from Its Quest to Build the Perfect Team," *New York Times Magazine*, February 25, 2016, https://www.nytimes.com/2016/02/28/magazine/what-google -learned-from-its-quest-to-build-the-perfect-team.html?_r=0. For an academic study on psychological safety on its influence on learning behavior in teams, see Amy Edmondson, "Psychological Safety and Learning Behavior in Work Teams," *Administrative Science Quarterly* 44, no. 2 (1999): 350–383.

15. These design principles are discussed in, e.g., Mark Wilson, "Logitech Quadrupled Its Profits — With One Big Design Idea," *Fast Company*, September 20, 2017, https://www.fastcompany.com/90143222/logitech-quadrupled-its-profits -with-one-big-design-idea.

16. See the following blog: Doug Powell, "A New Study on Design Thinking Is Great News for Designers," *Medium* (blog), March 14, 2018, https://medium .com/design-ibm/a-new-study-on-design-thinking-is-great-news-for-designers -593f71b40627.

17. Benjamin Brown, *The Total Economic Impact™ of IBM's Design Thinking Practice* (Cambridge, MA: Forrester Consulting, 2018).

18. Eli Meixler, "IBM Is Making Its Design Thinking Available to Clients, Says Its Design Chief," *Fortune*, March 7, 2018, http://fortune.com/2018/03/07/ibm -enterprise-design-thinking/.

19. Doug Powell, "A New Approach to Design Thinking," video filmed in January 2016 at the O'Reilly Design Conference 2016, San Francisco, California, https://www.youtube.com/watch?v=c0el19EKXYU&t=177s. For more information on the IBM design thinking program, termed "Enterprise Design Thinking," see https://www.ibm.com/design/thinking/.

20. Another example along similar lines with the IBM design thinking initiative can be found at General Electric: the "Menlo Innovation Ecosystem." During a series of multiday workshops, spread over a specific time period, internal teams engage and resolve real-world problems using design thinking approaches, tools, and techniques. More on the content of these workshop and how the program is structured can be found in Sarah J. S. Wilner, "Developing Design Thinking: GE Healthcare's Menlo Innovation Model," in *Design Thinking: New Product Development Essentials from the PDMA*, ed. Michael G. Luchs, Scott Swan, and Abbie Griffin (Hoboken, NJ: John Wiley & Sons, 2015): 157–172.

21. For more on how to create a design brief, see Peter L. Phillips, *Creating the Perfect Design Brief: How to Manage Design for Strategic Advantage* (New York: Allworth, 2012).

22. See, e.g., Bec Paton and Kees Dorst, "Briefing and Reframing: A Situated Practice," *Design Studies* 32, no. 6 (2011): 573–587.

23. See "Atlassian Design System," Atlassian, accessed February 22, 2021, https://atlassian.design/.

24. "What Is Carbon?" Carbon Design System, accessed February 22, 2021, https://www.carbondesignsystem.com/get-started/about-carbon.

25. Banfield, *Design Leadership*, 97.

26. For an easy-to-read blog on intrinsic versus extrinsic motivation, see, e.g., K. Cherry, "Differences of Extrinsic and Intrinsic Motivation," *Verywell Mind* (blog), January 15, 2020, https://www.verywellmind.com/differences-between-extrinsic-and-intrinsic-motivation-2795384. In this blog, a link to further readings is also provided. As explained in the blog, extrinsic and internal motivation interact with each other: extrinsic motivation can, for example, undermine intrinsic motivation. Furthermore, intrinsic motivation is not a fixed characteristic of an individual but is mutable, hence the need to carefully balance intrinsic and extrinsic motivators.

CHAPTER 7

1. For a broader, research-grounded overview of the advantages and disadvantages of these two approaches, see Helen Perks, Rachel Cooper, and Cassie Jones, "Characterizing the Role of Design in New Product Development: An Empirically Derived Taxonomy," *Journal of Product Innovation Management* 22, no. 2 (2005): 111–127; and Bettina Von Stamm, "Whose Design Is It? The Use of External Designers," *The Design Journal* 1, no. 1 (1998): 41–53.

2. Dylan Field, "6 Major Tech Companies Have Doubled Their Design Hiring Goals in Last Half Decade," *TechCrunch,* May 31, 2017, http://tcrn.ch/2qBJatt.

3. Esther Blankenship, "Meet Sam, Chief Design Officer at SAP," *SAP User Experience Community*, July 18, 2016, https://experience.sap.com/basics/meet-sam -chief-design-officer-at-sap/.

4. Tua Björklund, Hanna Maula, Sarah A. Soule, and Jesse Maula, "Integrating Design into Organizations: The Coevolution of Design Capabilities," *California Management Review* 62, no. 2 (2020): 100–124.

5. Ingo Rauth, Lisa Carlgren, and Maria Elmquist, "Making It Happen: Legitimizing Design Thinking in Large Organizations," *Design Management Journal* 9, no. 1 (2014): 47–60.

6. For an overview of these and other abilities of designers, see Ingo Karpen, Gerda Gemser, and Giulia Calabretta, "A Multilevel Consideration of Service Design Conditions," *Journal of Service Theory and Practice* 27, no. 2 (2017): 384–407.

7. For academic research on the importance of stimulating both the emotional and the rational in decision makers to influence their decisional outcomes, see Giulia Calabretta, Gerda Gemser, and Nachoem M. Wijnberg, "The Interplay Between Intuition and Rationality in Strategic Decision Making: A Paradox Perspective," *Organization Studies* 38, nos. 3–4 (2017): 365–401.

8. Paul Gardien, Maarten Rincker, and Eva Deckers, "Designing for the Knowledge Economy: Accelerating Breakthrough Innovation Through Co-Creation," *The Design Journal* 19, no. 2 (2016): 283–299.

9. Benjamin Brown, *The Total Economic Impact™ of IBM's Design Thinking Practice* (Cambridge, MA: Forrester Consulting, 2018).

CHAPTER 8

1. For a more in-depth discussion on the tension between creativity and commerce, see, e.g., Robert DeFillippi, Gernot Grabher, and Candace Jones, "Introduction to Paradoxes of Creativity: Managerial and Organizational Challenges in the Cultural Economy," *Journal of Organizational Behavior* 28, no. 5 (2007): 511–552; Manto Gotsi, Constantine Andriopoulos, Marianne Lewis, and Amy E. Ingram, " Managing Creatives: Paradoxical Approaches to Identity Regulation," *Human Relations* 63, no. 6 (2010): 781–805.

2. For a discussion about Pragmatism as a philosophy within the context of research on organizations, see, e.g., Moshe Farjoun, Christopher Ansell, and Arjen Boin, "Perspective — Pragmatism in Organization Studies: Meeting the Challenges of a Dynamic and Complex World," *Organization Science* 26, no. 6 (2015), 1787–1804.

3. Another literature stream that elaborates on dualities and is gaining more and more in popularity within the management literature adopts the so-called paradox lens. Literature adopting a paradox lens also suggests that long-term performance

requires continuous efforts to meet multiple, diverging demands. Thus, as suggested in this literature stream, rather than choosing between competing alternatives, long-term performance depends on engaging with them both. See, e.g., Wendy Smith and Marianne Lewis, "Toward a Theory of Paradox: A Dynamic Equilibrium Model of Organizing," *Academy of Management Review* 36, no. 2 (2011): 381–403; Wendy Smith, "Dynamic Decision Making: A Model of Senior Leaders Managing Strategic Paradoxes," *Academy of Management Journal* 57, no. 6 (2014): 1592–1623.

4. James Collins and Jerry Porras, *Built to Last: Successful Habits of Visionary Companies* (New York: HarperBusiness, 1997).

5. Roberto Verganti, Luca Vendraminelli, and Marco Iansiti, "Innovation and Design in the Age of Artificial Intelligence," *Journal of Product Innovation Management* 37, no. 3 (2020): 212–227.

6. Sylvia Von Wallpach, Benjamin Voyer, Minas Kastanakis, and Hans Mühlbacher, "Co-Creating Stakeholder and Brand Identities: Introduction to the Special Section," *Journal of Business Research* 70 (2017): 395–398.

7. Robin J. Ely and David A. Thomas, "Getting Serious About Diversity," *Harvard Business Review* (November- December, 2020): 114–122.

8. Fabrizio Ceschin and Idil Gaziulusoy, "Evolution of Design for Sustainability: From Product Design to Design for System Innovations and Transitions," *Design Studies* 47 (November 2016): 118–163.

Index

About the Authors

Eric Quint is former Senior Vice President, Chief Brand and Design Officer at 3M Company and former Vice President, Head of Design Management and Consulting at Royal Philips. In his role as the first Chief Brand and Design Officer at 3M, Eric was at the helm to scale brand and design across the global enterprise. During his tenure at 3M, he initiated and implemented a new corporate brand identity, designed and realized a state-of-the-art design center at the company headquarters, and opened several international design studios. With over twenty years of international roles in executive design leadership, he brings extensive experience in building and managing multidisciplinary creative teams to drive brand and innovation. He is a renowned design industry leader and a successful practitioner of design thinking as a mindset for transformation across multiple levels of an organization. Under Eric's design leadership and strategic vision, his design teams have been recognized with over 150 international design awards. He is a frequent keynote speaker and guest lecturer at international conferences and universities. His achievements are referenced and featured in numerous international books and publications. Eric studied industrial design at the Design Academy Eindhoven, the Netherlands, and holds a degree in mechanical and industrial engineering.

Gerda Gemser is Full Professor and Chair of (Corporate) Entrepreneurship in the Department of Management and Marketing at the University of Melbourne. She received her PhD in Management at the Rotterdam School of Management (Erasmus University, the Netherlands). Gerda was a visiting scholar at The Wharton School (University of Pennsylvania) and UBC Sauder School of Business (University of British Columbia). Previously she was Full (Research) Professor of Business & Design at the Royal Melbourne Institute of Technology. In addition, Gerda has held (assistant and associate) professorships at several Dutch universities, including Erasmus University, Delft University of Technology, and the University of Groningen. She collaborates with government, professional associations, and industry on various research projects investigating creativity, (corporate) entrepreneurship, and innovation. She teaches courses and gives seminars in these areas and is author or coauthor of over forty research articles, appearing in leading academic journals such as *Academy of Management Journal*, *Organization Science*, *Organization Studies*, *Journal of Management*, *Design Studies*, and *Journal of Product Innovation Management*. She is coauthor of *Strategic Design: Eight Essential Practices Every Strategic Designer Must Master* (2nd edition).

Giulia Calabretta is Associate Professor in Strategic Value of Design at the Faculty of Industrial Design Engineering at Delft University of Technology (the Netherlands). She received her PhD in Management Science from ESADE Business School (Spain) and held a postdoctoral position at BI Norwegian School of Management. Her research explores the intersection of (strategic) design, management, and innovation, and has been published in prominent academic journals, including *Organization Studies, Journal of Product Innovation Management*, and *Journal of Business Ethics*. She has collaborated in the writing of several book chapters and coauthored *Strategic Design: Eight Essential Practices Every Strategic Designer Must Master* (2nd edition). Giulia is currently involved in various research projects with public and private sector partners investigating how to grow innovation capabilities and how design can be leveraged for business and societal impact. She has taught strategic design, design leadership, and innovation management at several universities and executive education programs worldwide. As the director of the Master's Program in Strategic Product Design at Delft University of Technology, Giulia plays an active role in the creation of effective design leadership education for the future. She is frequently invited to be a keynote speaker at universities and business conferences, and in companies.